"Doris Dixon was t[here] in its very beginning[s] of us. It's hard to even begin to say how much we [owe her]."
—Cleveland Amory, Author of *The Cat Who Came for Christmas* and *Ranch of Dreams*

"Doris Dixon is one of the kindest people I know. And one of the toughest. But tough or kind, she is an inspiration to everyone engaged in the battle for animals."
—Tom Hennessy, Columnist, *Press Telegram*, Long Beach, CA

"This powerful and inspiring book, by one of America's best respected animal protectionists, is a 'must' read for anyone concerned about the future of our fellow creatures – and ourselves. Dixon has an amazing and fascinating story to tell."
—Lewis Regenstein, Author of *The Politics of Extinction* and *America The Poisoned*

"An account of a woman's life lived to its fullest, Doris Dixon retraces her girlhood loves, her wartime years in the Big Apple, and most compellingly of all, her growing sense of the importance of the animal kingdom. In spite of her prominence in some circles, it is all conveyed without a hint of snobbery, and the entire writing is beautifully but unpretentiously woven into the fabric of her life's tale. In truth, you don't have to care a whit about animals to fall in love with Doris, but it wouldn't hurt."
—Dr. Sidney Gendin, Professor of Philosophy, Eastern Michigan University

"A kind, gentle book from the heart of a similar woman who has shown so many of us how to turn our rage against animal cruelty into compassionate, productive effort. It's an easy read, at times very humorous and always informative. When I die, I won't be a bit surprised to discover God turns out to be Doris Dixon."
—Jerry Cesak, Creator of "Bless The Beasts"

Thanks for caring!
Doris Dixon
1999

Memoirs of a Compassionate Terrorist

Doris Dixon
with Carolyn Smith

Proctor Publications

© 1998 Doris Dixon, First Edition

Published in the USA by
Proctor Publications
PO Box 2498
Ann Arbor, MI 48106

All rights reserved.
No part of this book may be reproduced in any form
or by any means, except in the context of reviews,
without permission in writing from the author.

Library of Congress Card Catalog Number: 97–75370

Publisher's Cataloging-in-Publication
(Provided by Quality Books, Inc.)

Dixon, Doris.
Memoirs of a compassionate terrorist / Doris Dixon -- 1st ed.
p. cm.
ISBN 1-882792-56-4

1. Fund for Animals. 2. Dixon, Doris. 3. Animal rights activists--United States--Biography. I. Title.

HV4766.A2F86 1997	179'. 3092
	QBI97-41311

Dedicated to Todd and Koko

Acknowledgments

To Cleveland Amory and Marian Probst of The Fund for Animals, without whom I would have never had the opportunity to embark on this path; Lewis Regenstein; Carolyn and Gregory Smith; Tom Hennessy; Jerry St. James; Sing Song; Bobbi; ShadoE and TeTu; Doris Day, an inspiration; my parents, now passed on, for showing me the importance of caring for all God's creatures; E.R. Adams; Carol and Carl Akerloff; E. Dodman; Yanhia Gamero; Sidney Gendin; Carol Halstead; Joan Hill; A.F. Holter; Stephanie Hunter; Susan M. Kornfield; J. Louth; Jesse Richards; John Simecek; Jack and Jocelyn Sullivan; Amy Walsh; and the special staff of Proctor Publications.

Preface

Did you know that people working for animal rights typically lead normal lives and are not terrorists? Did you know that they can be found in all ages, genders, religions, political persuasions, races, social classes, and professions? Did you know that many of them may be your friends, neighbors, business associates, and others with whom you come in daily contact? If not, this book is for you. You may even recognize yourself within these pages and realize you are one of the millions uncomfortable with the way animals are treated in our society, yet who, like so many others, feel outnumbered and intimidated. *Memoirs of a Compassionate Terrorist* chronicles the coming of age of a social movement as seen through the eyes of Doris Dixon, Midwest Representative for The Fund for Animals, a woman who addresses the animal cause in a deeply dedicated, inspiring, and unique way, and who is not, by any means, a terrorist. In fact, she's pretty darn nice.

Introduction

The greatness of a nation and its moral progress can be judged by the way its animals are treated.
                                        –Gandhi

There have been attempts by the United States government, the media, and even some television sitcoms to portray those in the animal rights movement on a par with any of the FBI's "Most Wanted." Prior to the 1990 March for the Animals in Washington, D.C., former Health and Human Services Secretary Louis Sullivan referred to animals rights activists as terrorists, despite any proof of the accusation. Cleveland Amory, founder and president of The Fund for Animals, countered in his opening statement on the Capitol steps, "As Doris Dixon has aptly stated, 'How times have changed. They used to call people like me little old ladies in tennis shoes. Now I'm a *terrorist*.'"

To my knowledge, I have never known anyone remotely resembling a terrorist within the animal rights movement. Like other conscientious people, I don't consider exposing illegal or unethical animal dealings via peaceful protest or even civil disobedience as terrorism, but rather as long overdue acts on behalf of animals. It is interesting that as nonviolent as animal rights people are – no person having ever been harmed in their pursuits – the exploiters of animals often attempt to paint us as terrorists. What a challenge we must be to their consciences and pocketbooks that they label us in such a way while excusing their own actions. For example, hunters not only maim and kill their prey, but also innocent bystanders and often each other during their hunting escapades; neither they nor their apologists apparently consider such acts as terrorism.

This book is intended to help promote understanding of what it's like to be an activist for animals – who I am, what shapes my life, and why I'm dedicated to this effort. I hope to dispel the myths surrounding people devoted to the animal welfare/rights cause. We are much like you – kind, caring people involved in meaningful work. Hardly the "terrorists" we are sometimes portrayed as.

1
Having a Life

It is a matter of taking the side of the weak against the strong, something the best people have always done.
—Harriet Beecher Stowe

As our bus rounded the corner of the little all-American looking town of Hegins, Pennsylvania, my mind was crowded with thoughts of what we were about to witness. As part of The Fund for Animals' Michigan contingent, I had joined with hundreds of others from across the country, and indeed the world, to protest the yearly Hegins Labor Day pigeon shoot, the local idea of "fun." How ironic that the pigeon, cousin of the dove (Columbidea family), is demeaned by some as a "rat with wings," whereas most people regard the dove as a symbol of peace.

The scene at Hegins included men with beer (and bellies to match) lining up for a shot at pigeons who had been crowded into small crates for days, brought in from surrounding towns. Frightened and disoriented, the creatures were released, one at a time, for the locals to blast at, to the cheers of the spectators – many of them families with children present. Young boys dispatched any injured birds left flopping around. They did this by either stomping them to death or by pulling off their heads. For hours, our people rushed the field to delay the shoot or to retrieve injured birds. Several protesters were arrested for disorderly conduct and trespassing – while all around us, a massacre was legally taking place!

One of the saddest things one of our group witnessed that day was a young boy of about four or five who tried to avert his eyes from the carnage. A man beside him grasped him by the shoulders, forcing him to face the killing field. Despite the boy's continued efforts to turn away, the man held him firmly in place, apparently determined that "the family that slays together, stays together."

Toward mid-afternoon, three members of the Ku Klux Klan arrived, two of them in full white regalia. They stood in stone-faced silence, obviously there to offer their moral support to the slaughterers. Their presence alone should serve as a warning to anyone who believes such "sport" to be good, clean fun.

As the day drew to a close, one of the shooters approached our group and accused us of, among other things, "not having a life." Otherwise, so his reasoning went, we wouldn't be in Hegins on a holiday weekend, but rather at home enjoying ourselves. We could only wonder exactly what kind of life any of us would have if we were able to shut out these horrors and take it easy. Those of us in the animal rights movement have lives, and very fulfilling ones at that. We are from all walks of life – aware, caring people with a sense of commitment and, ironically, even of humor. At times, all we can do is laugh at life's endless absurdities while persistently trying to change things for the better.

While married to a Big Three auto executive in the fifties and sixties, the "good life" for me included business trips to Hawaii and vacations in locales far more inviting than Hegins. I was also part of the country club scene (an uncle of mine helped establish Ann Arbor's most prestigious country club).

I came to realize the absurdity of such a lifestyle when, shortly after my divorce, a friend invited me to have dinner at an area club. I was surprised to see many of the same people there that I had socialized with years before. As Peggy Lee asked in the title of her famous recording, "Is That All There Is?" Country clubs, yacht clubs, and nightclubs were fun for a time, but couldn't and didn't offer me what I needed to be truly fulfilled – namely, a humane sense of purpose. I have learned along the way that, as sad as so many aspects of the animal cause can be, it is indeed far more rewarding than any country club scene.

My "wake up call" came, quite literally, a few years before via the *Tonight Show*. I had dozed off on my couch after a long night of surveillance as a private investigator for a security company when I was awakened by a man talking about animals. He spoke eloquently of the plight of laboratory animals and other such atrocities. As one who had always loved animals, I was both impressed and moved by his words. So much, in fact, that the next day, I wrote to the show – a big deal for me at the time, since I seldom wrote letters – to find out who the guest was.

My inquiry was forwarded to The Fund's headquarters in New York City and I soon learned that the man was Cleveland Amory: author, television critic, founder, and unpaid president of The Fund for Animals. My interest was further piqued by the organization's mission: "to speak for those who can't." I couldn't resist calling the New York office. I first spoke with Marian Probst, Cleveland's longtime assistant, who then asked me, as if it were an everyday event, if I'd like to speak to Cleveland. I did and I soon found myself with a new, yet somehow deeply ingrained, calling – that of helping the helpless.

Before establishing The Fund for Animals in 1967, Cleveland Amory was best known as a social historian and author, having written such bestsellers as *Who Killed Society?*, *The Proper Bostonians*, *The Last Resorts*, and more recently, *The Cat Who Came for Christmas* and *Ranch of Dreams*. He also served as a contributing writer for *Saturday Review* and *Parade* magazines, as well as media critic for *TV Guide*.

During a trip to Mexico in the mid-sixties, Cleveland's humanity was put to the test when urged by friends to attend the local "sport" – a bullfight. When the "victorious" matador finally paraded his trophy – a bloody bull's ear – before the roaring crowd, Cleveland could take it no more. He rushed to the front row of seats and pelted the "hero" with a seat cushion, heavy and soggy from recent rains.

As he later described the "sport", "If you have the misfortune to attend a bullfight, for every bull you see with even a nodding acquaintance with fearsome qualities, you will see at least three whose only desire, on leaving their darkened enclosure and entering, half-blinded by the light, an arena filled with a screaming, bloodthirsty mob, is not to fight but merely to find a way out. The *aficionado* who adores telling you how the brave bull can beat a lion or tiger has never shown the slightest inclination to get into the ring with any other kind of animal, from a guard dog to a cross goose."

When I first spoke with Cleveland, he was unaware of

my background as a private investigator. Nevertheless, call it fate or second sight, he asked if I would be willing to look into a few animal-related problems in the Midwest. As a new volunteer, I was apprehensive, but he assured me that "in two months, you'll know as much as anyone in the country." Sure enough, in a short time, I did know more about the animal cause than most people. That was really frightening. It didn't mean I was exceptionally smart, but rather how little most people knew about what was happening to animals, sometimes literally in their own backyards.

One of my first assignments for The Fund was to investigate a suspicious animal exploitation business in southeastern Michigan. A friend of Cleveland's operated an airline in Miami whose business was used to transport large cats from around the world to hunting preserves in South America. Ever the private eye, I posed as a middle-aged floozy (complete with outlandish wig and toreador pants), accompanying a young paramour, actually one of my fellow detectives, who was interested in adopting a wild cat as a "pet." After talking to the company's owner, we discovered that their warehouse was the transportation hub for animals they procured in Africa and elsewhere. From there, they routed them to zoos, movie lots, research labs, and hunting safari clubs. They also owned pet shops as well as travel agencies that offered (surprise!) hunting safaris to South America.

After acquiring this information, we realized prosecution would be difficult since businesses like this often creep along a fine line between legal and illegal activities. However, Tom Hennessy, then a *Detroit Free Press* columnist, used the results of our investigation to help write a series of newspaper exposes. He continued to write outstanding articles on other aspects of animal rights, as well. One of the first was a feature article about me in the Sunday magazine section of the *Detroit Free Press*, which resulted in gaining many recruits for the cause. In a personal letter, he later acknowledged, "If it were not for you, I might be out in the woods right now in an orange vest – perish the thought!"

Tom Hennessy was later among the first, along with Abigail Van Buren of "Dear Abby" and Charles Schulz of "Peanuts," to receive one of the Genesis Awards (established by The Fund in 1986 and currently sponsored by The Ark Trust, Inc.), which honors "those in the media whose courage and integrity have increased public awareness of animal issues." Subsequent Genesis recipients include Hugh Downs, Paul Harvey, Garrison Keillor, Dr. Jane Goodall, Doris Day, Andy Rooney, Paul McCartney, and Jacques Cousteau, to name a few.

Thanks to such efforts by Tom and others in the media, many questionable dealings with animals have come to light, running the gamut from "canned hunts" where captive, sometimes human-trusting animals provide a guaranteed kill for the laziest of hunters, to the illegal trade in exotic and often endangered species.

Another of my early assignments was to investigate an animal "shelter" in southeastern Ohio, located approximately ten miles from the nearest town. Unwanted animals could simply be dropped down an outdoor chute into a cramped basement holding pen, apparently under the premise, "out of sight, out of mind". The abandoned animals were picked up twice weekly by the county animal control officer, whose wife just happened to be an animal dealer (meaning she was licensed to sell animals to labs for experimentation). After gathering sufficient evidence of cruelty and possible conflict of interest, I alerted the local authorities. They appeared unaware of this "stop and drop" method of animal disposal which had been taking place. Civic-mindedness, coupled with outraged public opinion, helped convince the county to join forces with The Fund to implement a more humane method of rescuing homeless animals.

I returned from that adventure with a "sassamutt" whom I named Pocahontas (PooKoo), a black and tan beagle-mix who cried so piteously from the so-called shelter's holding pen upon my first visit that I had no choice but to crawl into the dank chute and rescue her.

One of the endearing remembrances of life with PooKoo was how she would totally ignore me as I left for work fussing good-bye messages to her, so I would be certain to understand that leaving would be my loss, as well as hers. I also quickly learned, without a clock, when it was after 8 p.m., because she would not permit anyone to pet her after that point. She obviously had her rules and my son, Todd, and I simply had to abide by them. Because she was not pedigreed and was not always obedient, one person referred to her as a "nothing" dog. If she was a "nothing" dog, I'd sure like to see a "something" dog. Pook was in fact the smartest dog in the world; she chose to understand everything except "No."

Once comfortably settled into her routine, PooKoo became the official greeter at the door of my Fund home-office, a perfect role for one with her bouncy manner and genuine love of people, despite her negative experiences with some of them before coming to live with us. She even tolerated our family felines. Her goodwill was not, however, extended to our only other dog, a deaf Dalmatian named Pet.

Pet had come to us, or rather we to her, while I was on another of my early assignments in Ohio. When I first met her, she was nothing but fur over bones and two beautiful, pleading brown eyes. I couldn't get her out of my thoughts.

The family at the farmhouse where I had seen her claimed she was not theirs. They said she had just been hanging around for several weeks with their dog and they feared she had been eating their chickens. I suggested that she needed medical attention, although I realized she would probably not get it. I later phoned the family to say I would purchase her if they would feed her well until I was able to pick her up a couple of days later. This tactic worked and we soon found ourselves with a very sick Dalmatian we named Petula. It was several weeks before we realized Pet was deaf as well as being plagued by every type of worm imaginable. After six months of love and rehabilitation, we were unable to find an appropriate home for her except, of course, ours. We were delighted to have her with us, although we would never fully understand why she dashed to the window whenever car headlights flashed by, seemingly longing for someone she missed who never came.

Fifteen years passed. In our eyes, Pet remained the most beautiful dog we'd ever seen. Her only shortcoming was her unpredictability; she would sometimes snap at other people or animals, primarily due to her deafness. She would also draw away in fear when anyone touched her ears or her paws. As Pet approached her teens, her health began to fail and she could no longer indulge in her favorite game of Frisbee. Medications were finally of no help. Despite the physical pain she endured toward the end, her last two days were filled with every joy dear to her heart. Todd spent every moment by her side. True to her Dalmatian heritage, she insisted on claiming her rightful spot in the front seat of his GMC Jimmy till the very end. Heaven is going to have to be awfully good to compare with her last days with those of us who loved her.

2
Different Hats

I am only one
But still I am one.
I cannot do everything.
But still I can do something:
And because I cannot do everything
I will not refuse to do the something that I can do.
–Edward Everett Hale

No stranger to the working world, I held a variety of jobs before, during, and after my marriage. These were as diverse as my many interests and included stints with the airlines, in the legal and advertising professions, and even as an Assistant Deputy City Treasurer for Ypsilanti, Michigan. Next to the animal cause, my most satisfying calling was as an investigator for a private security agency, where I handled a wide variety of cases, including missing persons and child custody.

One of my most memorable assignments was serving on the local security contingent for President John F. Kennedy when he visited Ann Arbor in 1960. It was there on the campus of the University of Michigan that he first presented his revolutionary plan to establish a civilian Peace Corps. A photograph of the President and our security force was published in the August 1962 issue of the *CII (Council of International Investigators)* journal. Of those in the photo, our head of security described me as "one of the best pistol shots" on the force.

After Kennedy's assassination in 1963, former Vice President Lyndon Johnson served in his stead as guest speaker at the University of Michigan's 1964 commencement ceremony. Nerves were understandably frayed and security was extremely tight. I served on a local team assigned to protect the new president. I was inconspicuously seated among the crowd in the stadium bleachers, listening to a man in the row behind me wondering aloud how easily Johnson could be attacked because there did not seem to be much security. How surprised that gentleman would have been to know that the woman sitting in front of him was on assignment, complete with weapon!

In a lighter vein, I got to "case the joint" for the famous Pretzel Bell restaurant in Ann Arbor. The owner hired our agents to visit the restaurant, then write up our experiences. What fun to sample the best of everything and to know that any comments we made would be taken very much to heart.

Then there was the "tic-tac-toe caper" or what was called "honesty shopping" in a chain of ice cream stores. To do this, I had to keep track of the waitperson's transactions, remembering the cash register amounts, before and after my purchases. In order to recall all the figures, it was important to write them down without the employee becoming suspicious.

My son Todd, then six years old, and I would play tic-tac-toe on a napkin while enjoying our sundaes, turning the napkin over to make notes when the waitperson was looking the other way. We did catch several persons "knocking down" (pocketing) money belonging to the business.

Bar checks were not as easy. It was necessary for me to sit at the bar (and have a drink, of course, to legitimize being there) and keep tabs on the bartender. Here again, I caught several wrongdoers by using the back of the napkin trick, but I had to keep my wits about me while imbibing.

Another surveillance trick of the trade was to safely change drivers while traveling down the road. Since the people my partner and I followed might wonder why the same car seemed to always be behind them, we would occasionally change drivers. That way, instead of seeing a man at the wheel, there was now a woman. This, plus wig changes and the like, helped us to maintain our high success rate.

Being a good private eye had to have been the result of preferring to work in the background. I have always tried to maintain a low profile, yet I keep finding myself up front. Even when graduating from junior high and extremely uncomfortable with the limelight, I was chosen to give the class speech. Although the presentation was successful, to this day I remain uncomfortable with public speaking and seek other ways to make my mark.

As a Fund representative, I am proud of the public recognition I have received for my contributions to many books and articles, such as *Mankind? Our Incredible War on Wildlife* and *The Cat and the Curmudgeon*, both by Cleveland Amory, and *The Politics of Extinction*, *America the Poisoned*, and *Replenish the Earth*, all by Lewis Regenstein.

Never was my ambivalence over my public vs. private

persona more apparent than when a supply of new Fund stationery arrived at my home-office one day. My husband, Tom, examined it, then asked if I knew who was on the new Fund Board of Directors. I replied, "Yes, Doris Day. Isn't that wonderful!" He then pointed out that directly under her name was my own. (Cleveland calls us his "two favorite Dorises"). To this day, she and I remain allies in the struggle on behalf of animals.

In this seemingly neverending struggle, I seldom have to find problems – they come to me. I characterize this as the "Why doesn't someone. . ." phenomenon, that "someone" usually being me. Fortunately, I have learned to delegate at least some responsibility and to motivate others, two musts if one is to avoid burnout. It is also vital to maintain credibility by staying well-informed on animal rights issues.

There are crackpots aplenty already out there taking their frustrations out on the animal rights movement. An area rock star/recently-turned disc jockey once characterized The Fund as a bunch of "Animal Rights Nazis" (a phrase which the verbally challenged interject when they can't think of anything intelligent to say). Shortly after his radio tirade, I began receiving threatening phone calls at home. I talked to my son who was living in Hawaii at the time. He reassured me, "Mom, if anyone ever comes after you, their own hatred will trip them up."

Although I initially worked on several cases for The Fund, it was a number of months before I finally had the chance to personally meet Cleveland. He was scheduled to speak at Northwood Institute and Town Hall in Midland, Michigan, some one hundred and fifty miles north of Ann Arbor. It was a more-miserable-than-usual Michigan winter's day, with roads snow-covered and slick and visibility approximately zero.

Fortunately, one of my friends, Chuck, volunteered to do the driving. After a harrowing trip, I found myself pumped up for the big moment – finally meeting my mentor. Cleveland and I felt an instant rapport. After a day in the company of educators and socialites, we spent most of the evening talking about – what else? – animals. Cleveland later wrote to thank me for my "yeoman work." I was just beginning to understand how *much* work, and gratification, I would have with The Fund. Much to my surprise, he also referred to me as "our Number One hope in the Midwest."

Cleveland later recalled, "When I founded The Fund for Animals in 1967, we had only hope and $900 in hand. But I felt then that our cause would probably succeed and our success would be enhanced, because we had, besides this $900, an inestimable advantage. We soon had Doris on our staff. She became our first coordinator and she has been our senior staff member ever since. And, for all of that tumultuous time, she has been firm as a rock, strong as Gibraltar, wise as an owl, consistently constructive, and one of the best friends The Fund for Animals, and the animals themselves, have probably ever had. What we say at The Fund is, if you have a question, ask Doris, because she knows everything. And since she knows everything, she knows we love her."

One of the first Detroit television appearances I scheduled for Cleveland necessitated my driving from my home to the Dearborn Inn where he was staying, and from there to the WXYZ TV studio in Southfield. It was early morning, rush hour traffic, and pouring rain to boot. As I exited the freeway, I had a flat tire. A good Samaritan stopped to help and, despite my obvious safety concerns, I trusted that all would work out – it had to. I accepted his gracious offer of a ride to Cleveland's hotel. From there, we caught a taxi and made it to the TV appearance just in time.

A similarly hair-raising experience was having Cleveland call me one day during my lunch break from my "day job" as a secretary at Washtenaw Community College. According to him, I needed to be in Dayton, Ohio by 6 p.m. A dinner was being held for him and he needed my help ("and bring brochures – lots of them"). I don't know how, but I did it. I washed my hair, made plane reservations and threw together a wardrobe to cover both the evening banquet as well as Cleveland's appearance, which I had arranged, on the *Phil Donahue Show* the following morning. Fortunately, I had chosen my clothing carefully. When I was unexpectedly asked by Cleveland to stand up in the Donahue audience, I could model our newest fundraising animal-motif skirt. It had been designed by Dollie Cole, wife of the president of General Motors, an animal welfare advocate and friend of one of The Fund's board members.

Throughout my years with The Fund, I have served in many capacities. As I once explained on Detroit's WJR radio, "My first title was Midwest Representative. I asked Cleveland, 'What's that?' and he replied, 'That's everything between the East Coast and the West Coast.'" One of my earliest assignments was to set up a Fund office in Chicago. Despite challenging conditions (cramped office space, no bathroom nearby, unwelcoming area of town), a small band of volunteers and I succeeded beyond all expectations.

One of these volunteers, Felicite Buhl, became a close friend. She had just retired as an editor at Encyclopedia Britannica and was anxious to help animals in whatever way she could. She felt sorry for me, living in that tiny office for days at a time. She would often pick me up in her little VW, take me to dinner, and then to her nice apartment in Park Ridge, where I could sleep in luxury. I also got to enjoy the companionship of her darling Siamese, Shin Dong. She had discovered Shin one night, skinny and dirty, under her car in the apartment garage. Felicite and I had great times plotting strategies, calling talk shows, and sharing our expertise. Years later, when Felicite passed away, she left a portion of her estate, as well as her indefatigable spirit, to The Fund.

Another special volunteer and friend was Colette Faber. When I first met her, she seemed very dignified and reserved. I couldn't help wondering if she was up to the rigors of animal rights work. However, she dug right in with enthusiasm and common sense. As she became aware of the many horrors inflicted upon animals, she became even more determined in her actions and far less "ladylike" with her language. Her mother, an equally dedicated woman, helped to handle the merchandising of our fundraising items. Colette was also very skillful at working with the media. She held things together in Chicago for several years. Colette, too, has passed on, but her dedication to animals and to The Fund continues to hold many wonderful memories for those of us who worked alongside her.

For nearly a year, while setting up the new Chicago office, I spent extended weekends at home. Heaven to me was returning from my Chicago jaunts to the welcome of my son and our companion animals – a major part of my support system. The walks on the hard concourse at O'Hare Field, carrying two heavy suitcases full of literature and other work, were really tough. Often I would take the train home just to have the time to read my mail. It was rough going, but the animals inspired me and I was proud to be part of such an effort.

One of Cleveland's rare letters to me from Washington, D.C. during this period expresses the sense of urgency and hopefulness that we all shared. "Sorry, sorry, sorry that I'm such a bad correspondent, but there's such a deluge of mail here from people who want me, among other things, to stop the slaughter of baby seals, that I just count on your understanding. At that, I think we may be getting somewhere. One group is going to picket the Canadian Consulate here. Others have been plaguing the Canadian Tourist Board. This is the first year The Fund has been able to afford to have an observer actually on the ice. I have a lot of faith in him. You are a dear. Thanks for all you have done and are doing."

The Fund's observer documented on film the many cruelties involved in sealing: the clubbing of baby seals, the skinning of the sometimes still-living creatures, the mother seals watching helplessly. Determined to stop this slaughter, Cleveland launched an expedition to "paint" as many baby seals as possible with a permanent red organic dye. This tactic was harmless to the seals, who would shed their baby fur as they matured, but devastating to hunters who were after the pure white fur. With the advice and help of longtime Fund for Animals' friend and experienced ship's captain, Paul Watson, The Fund purchased an old North Sea trawler, the *Sea Shepherd*. Eighteen tons of concrete were poured into the ship's bow to enable it to break through the nearly impenetrable pack ice it would encounter on its way to the seal herd.

After nearly a week of rough going, the *Sea Shepherd* arrived at its destination in Hudson Bay. As the trawler plowed its way through the ice floes, the crew at *port* bow could see the skinned carcasses of baby seals, their grieving mothers moaning nearby. On the *starboard* bow, however, the surviving babies could be seen playing in the moonlight. Nearly the entire crew, including Cleveland, leapt onto the ice to witness this miracle of survival. Meanwhile, volunteers donned survival suits and, equipped with heavy canisters of red dye, fanned out swiftly over the ice. By morning, they had painted over one thousand seals! The Canadian Coast Guard, guardian of the slaughterers, finally realized what was happening and sent helicopters to track down the painters and arrest them. One of the *Sea Shepherd* volunteers described his experience to the media. "Most of the night was methodical – search the ice for pups without falling in. I spend a few minutes with a pup, trying to comfort him. He expects to be murdered, turns his head away, and cringes. I gently splash some dye from my bottle on his back and rub it in. I tell him that not all humans do the terrible things he has seen in his first few days and that we are trying to stop the horror."

No matter how successful an animal rights mission may be, it can only contribute to a broader social awareness if the public knows of it. To insure that the horrors of the seal slaughter were brought to light, Dick Cavett, a fellow board member at the time (as well as host of the *Tonight Show*) asked me after one of his shows I had attended, if I could suggest someone to discuss the seal issue on his program. I told him I felt there was no one better than Amory for the task, and Cavett urged me to have Cleveland call him. The next day, I must have reminded Cleveland three or four times to call Cavett (as though anyone would forget such an invitation).

Cleveland's appearance on the *Tonight Show* provided the first late night national exposure of the seal kill, complete with graphic pictures from the "front lines." Thereafter, while our other forces were on the ice, our local efforts were focused on petitioning, leafletting and education, as well as radio and TV interviews. These efforts paid off. The public outcry helped convince the Canadian government to significantly reduce the quota of seal pups in particular. We had won a battle, but not the war. Thinking that such massive attention would sustain improvements, activists turned their efforts toward other imminent animal problems. Unfortunately, once out of the public eye, the Canadians have quietly but surely increased their seal "harvest".

People must understand that *animal exploiters never give up*. They may lay low until public pressure is off, but they will most certainly rear their ugly heads again and again – necessitating constant vigilance.

Well aware of the continued dangers man poses to animals, *Sea Shepherd* captain Paul Watson went on to found the Sea Shepherd Conservation Society. He continues to wage an aggressive fight on behalf of all marine mammals, from seals to whales, and heads a fleet of ships, one of which he named the *Cleveland Amory*.

A bit closer to home, a somewhat unsettling experience occurred when I was picking up reprints of a newspaper article which pitted me against the former head of Michigan United Conservation Clubs (MUCC – in some ways an appropriate acronym). In what should be considered a conflict of interest, this person also served simultaneously for a time as the president of the National Rifle Association. The clerk at the print shop said, "I see you don't think much of hunting." He went on to explain that he worked part-time at Big Louie's (a local hunting ranch where hunters could pop off big game for big bucks and which was featured in the 1975 CBS hunting documentary, "Guns of Autumn"). "You know Louie is after you, don't you?" he asked. I calmly replied, "Sure, everyone knows that. We're just waiting for him." I hoped that if Louie was told this, he might realize that if I were harmed, he would be a prime suspect. A month or so later, two of Louie's brothers received prison sentences for plotting to kill someone with a car bomb. After that, I was pretty careful where I parked.

Former Fund vice president Lewis Regenstein has characterized me as "the toughest guy in the whole damned Fund." I once astonished the good old boys on the gun range by scoring a perfect ten while qualifying for a gun permit renewal. Early in my career as a private investigator, I held a membership as (at that time) the first and only female in the Washtenaw County Law Enforcement Association. At one Association gathering of approximately one hundred members, a guest speaking Circuit Court judge delivered the unusual salutation, "Gentlemen . . . [pause] . . . and Lady," while turning his attention to me. So much for the image of animal lovers as "little old ladies in tennis shoes." As Cleveland often observes, "They now have cleats on those shoes."

The Fund is active nationally and internationally, but it is first and foremost a grassroots movement. Charity does indeed begin at home, for if we can't change that with which we are most familiar, there is little hope of alleviating suffering on a regional, much less global, scale.

In my home state of Michigan, I helped eliminate the cruel, antiquated, and wasteful bounty on coyotes, long a favorite target animal for hunters and trappers. I worked with many individuals and humane societies to raise public awareness and to influence the state legislature to declare dogfighting a felony in Michigan. This particular blood sport uses live kittens as training bait and often forces the dogs to fight to death.

Dog racing profit-interests persistently try to introduce greyhound gambling/animal abuse into Michigan. They invariably meet with strong opposition, both because of the cruelty the dogs endure at human hands, and because, despite industry denials, the dogs are often trained on live rabbits and kittens. Although there are several organizations which attempt to place former racing greyhounds in good homes, this is only a band-aid approach to the larger problems. Eliminating the source of overbreeding and cruelty – words synonymous with the racing industry itself – is the only way to protect the greyhound. For all their service, once a dog is no longer a winner, and few are for long, many are shot to death, sold to labs for experimentation or left to starve by those who had hoped to get fat off them.

So many animals have to be euthanized in humane societies each year. In a way, these are the lucky ones because they won't face death by starvation, murder, disease, accidents or deliberate human cruelty. Indeed, humane societies are forced to do the daily dirty work for irresponsible humans. No one should allow his or her animal to breed simply so children may witness the "miracle of birth" – unless they are prepared to take those same children to the humane society to witness the miracle of death. There just aren't enough homes for all the animals, purebred, pedigreed or not. Everyone should be required to spend at least one day at a humane society. Perhaps then they would get the message that *pet overpopulation is a moral crime and one for which only the innocent are punished.*

While serving on the Board of Directors of my area humane society, I helped to institute the second low-cost spay and neuter clinic in the nation, despite opposition from some veterinarians who viewed this as a threat to their livelihood. I also worked to ban the decompression chamber, which had been used in some Michigan humane societies. This form of euthanasia, in which animals are slowly and painfully asphyxiated while the oxygen is pumped out of the chamber, was replaced with the more humane method of lethal injection. Still, there is no good way to kill an animal whose only "sin" is being born.

It is not just the overbreeding of domestic animals which results in cruel and unnecessary death. During the eighties, The Fund and others in the community successfully challenged the Detroit Zoo's policy of overbreeding certain species to ensure an abundant supply of cute babies to attract paying customers. That tactic inevitably led to a surplus of animals who were euthanized or sold either to other zoos or for research. Regarding its policy on euthanasia, the Detroit Zoo actually compared itself to a humane society, although humane societies obviously don't breed their own problems. As Cleveland Amory argues, "We're talking about animals who are prisoners for no other reason than they are what God made them."

Zoos use conservation to make confined cruelty.
Let's free the beasts and save the wilderness instead.
In the process, we might discover ourselves.
–BBC Wildlife Magazine

Within the last few years, a change in zoo directors and a commitment to listening to public opinion have resulted in many improvements at the Detroit Zoo.

3
In the Beginning

Do not forget that the world is one great family.
—Shinto Precept

    A great deal of my personal strength came from my family. My father's family was among the first pioneers of Ann Arbor Village. My grandfather, John Schumacher, was nationally recognized for his involvement in the United States temperance effort in the 1880s. He owned Schumacher Hardware, which stood on South Main Street, between William and Liberty Streets in downtown Ann Arbor. After retirement, his six sons, John Jr., Eddie, Franky, Robert (my dad), Burt, and Phillip took over the business. I had one sibling, Robert Jr., who was six years older than me and who is now deceased.

    For the first fourteen years of my life, I lived at 1421 West Huron Street, which still stands. Our four-bedroom brick home, built for our family, was wonderful. It had a sun deck upstairs and a sun porch downstairs, making it a home full of light and warmth. I particularly enjoyed our breakfast nook, which was cozy and smelled invitingly of home baking (and where, if I was late for breakfast, I would have to climb over my brother while he took the opportunity to try to trip me). A crystal chandelier hung in the dining room, a room used for everything from Mom's wonderful dinners to Dad's weekly poker club games (where I first learned the skill of outwitting the other guy).

I remember our backyard with its huge trees and a doubleglider swing for playing on with friends and, later, for fledgling courting rituals. Our basement included both a fruit cellar filled with Mom's canned goods and a large playroom (although to me, the entire house and grounds were for playing). We lived on a main thoroughfare, two houses from the Jackson Road/Dexter Avenue split. In the very early days, streetcars ran that route, although I only recall cars as our mode of transportation. We also had home delivery of milk.

Being born a redhead undoubtedly influenced my personality. When I was a small child, I was called a "redheaded woodpecker" by my playmates. Instead of feeling intimidated or isolated, I became increasingly confident of myself. When I came to understand that we owned our property, I would often block our sidewalk with the aid of a clothespole. In another tradition of my own making, I would lay low under our front hedge and spray passersby with a squirt gun on their way to the fairgrounds. They couldn't imagine what hit them – probably suspecting a dog relieving itself since the pistol was deliberately loaded with warm water!

Another early memory was sleeping in the downstairs sun porch while listening to the scary *Hermit's Cave*, a Sunday night radio thriller. Everyone else was upstairs sleeping. Our neighbor would often ask Mom, "Isn't she scared?" to which I would scoff and Mom would just reply, "No, she loves it." To this day, I prefer thought-provoking drama that offers a perspective different from the status quo.

My family always had cats, dogs, and even birds, all remembered with adoration. There were collies, Buddy and Pal, when I was a toddler. They followed me everywhere, especially while I was learning to walk, undoubtedly to keep a wary eye on me. Then there was my Boy, a Doberman who bit the mailman's pants (while he was wearing them, of course), walked me to school each day, and after a second mailman bite, had to be given to friends who lived in the country. That broke my heart, although we often visited him on our friends' farm. Not a mailman in sight out there, nor a beloved child to protect.

When I was three or so, my Mom's tiger cat had a litter of kittens. I was allowed to keep one. That meant choosing which ones would be given to new homes. I began by process of elimination, handing over the first kitten (the one I judged to be the least pretty). Immediately, my heart sank and I wanted her back. Somehow, the least pretty became the most important one to me. After that episode, Mom became a strong supporter of spaying and neutering animals, realizing there would never be enough homes for them all.

One of our dearest cats was Silvertip, a silver Persian. When he was only a few years old, he was accidentally struck and killed by a Michigan State Police car. The night before the accident, Mom told me of a dream she had that someone in uniform came to our door, holding either me or Silvertip in their arms, dead. She could not determine in her nightmare which one of us it was and urged me to be especially careful the next day. She was understandably shaken by both the dream and the subsequent reality, but she was also typically philosophical about it. After all, as she pointed out, there are many things in life which seem inexplicable, but which do have a reason. We just aren't always open to the message.

After the loss of Silvertip, Mom took me to the humane society where there was a recent litter. I viewed the four or five precious kittens and selected the one who hung back and appeared to have a watering eye. He seemed the most needy and to me the most special. I named him Bingo and together we enjoyed many years and lessons of love.

Skeeter, another dear family feline, was my companion when I was an adolescent. After sharing twelve remarkable years, he disappeared one night. We lived on a busy street, but Skeeter always avoided it, having once had a close call with a car. Our backyard, which abutted the former Ann Arbor Masonic Temple, had seemed a safe haven; that is until Skeeter unexpectedly disappeared. Calls to the humane society and to the police revealed nothing. We later discovered that Skeeter had been mistakenly picked up as a stray by the Temple's night watchman and taken to a veterinarian whom the city surreptitiously paid to euthanize unwanted animals. The vet obviously felt no obligation to check either the Lost and Found column in the local paper or to call the humane society (both of which we had notified of our loss) before executing his victims. Astonished and angered by this secretive and destructive policy, I protested to the city as well as to the newspaper – one of my earliest efforts at making public the atrocities committed against animals.

My parents provided me with a strong sense of personal responsibility for humans and animals alike. For example, my mother always took care of any neighborhood strays, feeding them and trying to find them good homes. At the very least, she saw to it that they were taken to the humane society rather than being left to roam the streets. She and my dad also helped anyone who stopped at our door seeking a meal or money in return for helping with household chores. In those days, the country's economy was very precarious and my parents did their best to help those who were down on their luck. I remember helping Mom with church suppers as well as preparing and delivering food and clothing baskets for people less fortunate than we were.

Our holiday meals were always quite festive and included friends and relatives as well as college students who had no one else to spend the occasion with. Some of my family's special friends were the Mortensons, the contractors for the University of Michigan football stadium, which was then under construction. They often stayed at our home when they were in town. So did C.J. Smith from Ohio, a corporate lawyer and football recruiter for University of Michigan. Growing up with such ties to the university athletic community, I became quite an avid fan of "The Victors," particularly of Tom Harmon, who received the 1940 Heisman trophy.

When very young, I was delighted to have the run of the sporting goods inventory of my family's store. I loved playing baseball and other sports with the neighborhood boys. I also loved to don my Superman cape and jump from our front porch – not a very long drop, fortunately. Another of my favorite activities was climbing the large tree in our backyard where I would perform acrobatics, such as hanging upside down by my knees. During one such escapade, I lost my balance and fell flat on the ground, knocking myself unconscious. On my way down, all I could think about was my cat who had just been standing beneath the tree, watching and perhaps worrying. I was so afraid I would fall on him, which, mercifully, I didn't. When I regained consciousness, my relief at finding him safe made my injuries seem rather insignificant.

On Sunday mornings, my dad would often take me to La Casa, a small candy and restaurant-type place on the corner of Main Street and East Liberty, near our hardware store. One morning, while having a chocolate soda there, a man at a nearby table kept watching me. People often stared because of my red hair, but this time I became increasingly uncomfortable with the unwanted attention. The man finally approached our table and apologized, telling my Dad that I reminded him of his little daughter who had recently died. I'll never forget that. It helped me understand why people sometimes behave the way they do.

Until about the age of five, I didn't particularly care about or notice the need for a greater sense of compassion in my life. I, like most children, cared for my family, pets, and friends, but not much for the world outside my immediate sphere. It was only when I developed a nearly fatal case of appendicitis and peritonitis that I came to better appreciate the suffering of others. I remember lying in a hospital bed in a great deal of pain with six drainage tubes in my belly. It took all of my energy to be nice to anyone, except for one nurse I liked a lot and one girl who was very sick, too. She seemed so lonely and frightened that I tried my best to be kind and supportive to her. I think this early brush with near-death helped make me more conscious of those who need to be cared for. Now, as an adult, I direct much of my energy toward animals. They are most often at humankind's mercy, without voices of their own to plead their cases.

After my hospital stay, one of my favorite childhood games was to perfect my nursing skills on the family cats, delivering their meals on special plates, etc. I also enjoyed playing office, endlessly shuffling papers and organizing things, no doubt influenced by my family's involvement in their business. Years later, as a Fund for Animals agent, these two skills would hold me in good stead.

Anyone who knows me can testify that I have never been one to sit still for long. Among my many activities were dancing lessons, which I began at age six. After years of practice and determination, I appeared in the annual "Juniors on Parade" at the Lydia Mendelssohn Theater. I went on to teach ballroom dancing as a teenager and won a number of dance contests after graduation from high school. This talent would later lead to a career opportunity that many young women only dream of: to try out for the New York City chorus line of the Rockettes.

As a typically self-conscious adolescent, one of my primary concerns was that I was cursed with a "Marilyn Monroe walk." I worked very hard to correct it, although in later years, I sometimes wished I had it back. Too soon old, too late smart. Even at that, I received a junior high gym class award for having the "best, most graceful" walk.

Horseback riding was another strong interest of mine. I used to frequent Mullison's stables at the old Fairgrounds (now Veterans' Park). Although I was severely allergic to horses, I couldn't resist being around them. When I was about eight, I began riding lessons. It was great, even though I experienced being thrown, run away with, and stepped on, though not, fortunately, all at the same time. I learned firsthand that when a horse realizes someone is under his hoof, he will lift up. Once I fell off my horse while riding with several friends. I saw many hooves pass over me. Then one landed right in the middle of my back, strong enough to leave a hoofprint. Had he not lifted up immediately upon impact, my back would surely have been broken.

I came to pity stable horses. With different people riding them daily, they get so many mixed messages. How I wished to have my own horse. In later years, I was, in a sense, able to call many rescuees my own on The Fund for Animals' Black Beauty Ranch in Texas. This one thousand acre refuge is home to many animals (horses, burros, goats, elephants, kittens, and even chimpanzees) who have been mistreated or abandoned by the humans they so faithfully served. Cleveland Amory's newest book, *Ranch of Dreams*, details the life of this wonderful project and the animals who have found a safe haven there.

4
So Much for Mike

We must not expect too much from men.
It is the dog that stands for fidelity and sacrifice.
The best part of man is the dog in him.
—Dio Lewis

Those of us in the animal rights movement are sometimes accused of not caring for people or, at the very least, of harboring a dislike for the opposite sex. For those who might share this misconception, characterizing me as a man-hater who cares only for animals, I have decided to relate a number of my relationships. The fact is, I like and love a great many people. I just don't like "jerks."

Beginning in junior high, there were infatuations. I went for the uniform. A very special boyfriend at the time was a bicycle messenger for Western Union. Later in life, during wartime, I dated a number of servicemen.

When I was in high school, I was a hall monitor. One day, a handsome young man in uniform entered the school. We chatted a while before I encouraged him to leave, as was part of my duties. The "uniform" was from West Point. He stopped by for several days while he was home on break. I finally began to tire of him since I had already set my sights on a boy in one of my classes. Before returning to the Point, the "uniform" asked me to a formal dance there. I declined, but encouraged him to invite a friend of mine. I later read in the society column about the big West Point event in which my friend was this guy's date. I felt quite left out, although I realized it was my own darned fault.

Then there was "Rob,"* whom every girl in high school found most attractive. He dated the most gorgeous girl in school and was considered off-limits. However, in time, Rob and I began occasionally dating. I loved his hair, which was cut just below his ears, brushed back, with a single wave falling to his forehead. At this time, the short butch (Army style) haircut came into fashion. Rob knew that I hated it, as I hated hornrimmed glasses and cigars. Well, he was daring, and so for fun one night, he asked me to pick him up in front of Nichols Arcade, a popular campus landmark. When I did, there he stood with his new brush cut, a cigar, and hornrimmed glasses. That did it! I thought if he cared so little about me, he wasn't worth it. He probably thought that if such superficial things mattered to me, I didn't care enough. My sense of humor about life and love had obviously not kicked into full gear at that point.

In my sophomore year of high school, I had a yen for "Bill," a big-shot junior on the swim and football teams. He was a catch, but he didn't give me the time of day, even though

---

*Names in quotations have been changed.

I sat directly across from him in homeroom. I carried that unfulfilled crush for about a year when, one evening, I walked into school for some event and the only other person in the hall was Bill. He finally noticed me and asked me for a date. That was a thrill, but having been ignored for a year took off some of the polish.

Other fun memories of high school include the night I left my slip at a male friend's family cottage. There was a large group of kids there, male and female. Most of the guys were on the football team. Although we all privately changed our clothes to go swimming, forgetting my slip at the cottage that night became the "scandal" at school. Even the football coach (a really great guy) teased me about it.

In the late forties, Mom rented upstairs rooms in our house. One of our roomers was Louis, a University of Michigan medical student from a prominent family in Rio de Janeiro. He was very personable and I would occasionally go to a movie with him. Louie often presented me with orchids by the dozen, shipped up from his country. It never dawned on me that he thought I now belonged to him. I'd never even kissed him. I did think it was nice, though, when he purchased a huge TV for my family's living room. What a surprise when he took his gift back after I dated a friend of his. Most of the girls I knew felt "Dr. Lou" was worth pursuing. But I realized I could never tolerate being with someone so possessive.

One of my earliest wartime romances was with Mike – a real charmer. When he first came to town, all the girls went for him. He was a Marlon Brando (circa Stanley in *A Streetcar Named Desire*) type: good-looking, carefree, and a terrific dancer. After we had dated a few times, Mike admitted that he only asked me for a date at first so his best friend could double with my best friend. I wasn't particularly surprised, since guys didn't always go for me right away; but if I cared for them, they usually ended up caring for me. Within three weeks, Mike was hooked. Mom was ever so smart where Mike was concerned. A mother always wants the perfect man for her daughter and, although Mike was very likable, he was too worldly for me. That romance remained hot and heavy for about a year, but Mom continued to shower so much attention on him that I finally got an overdose. So much for Mike.

Then there was Carl, whom I met just before he signed up with the Navy. I was heartbroken that he was going away. When he returned home on leave, he gave me a little Navy pin, which I treasured. On a trip to Minnesota with a girlfriend, I lost the pin on the Great Northern Railway. I wrote a heartrending letter to the railway, never dreaming that they could actually locate this little pin. I prayed – that's how much it meant to me. What a surprise when the pin was found and mailed to me by the railroad company. As big a crush as I had on this guy, it was fun to read my diary a couple of years later when every time he called me for a date, I refused. Fickle? Perhaps; or maybe I was just growing up.

As with many people, part of this growth process involved finding a special "home away from home," a place where I could spread my wings and at the same time feel safe. For me, Ocean City, Maryland, turned out to be just such a place. I first ventured there as a young adult to visit my best friend, Evelyn. She had taken a summer job at Jackson's Casino, a nightclub where her boyfriend, Hal, played saxophone during the summer. We stayed at his band's quarters, which consisted of several cottages. There was a young man staying with us, eating our food and even sleeping on one of our cots. We each thought he was someone else's friend, but after we got together to discuss it, we discovered that he was just some beach bum living off all of us.

It was a pretty fun life. I look back and wonder how I kept from losing my virtue. Lucky, I guess. And it helps to have personal values and determination. Do I think I missed anything? No. I enjoyed life more than most. I was just ever-so-particular about those with whom I shared my life. Was I tempted? I *still* hear the roar of the ocean!

Fun times they were: the boardwalk, the ocean in moonlight, and the "one-armed bandits" outside the club where we occasionally hit the jackpot. And speaking of jackpots, upon my first visit to Jackson's, I noticed a tall, blond Greek-god type descending the balcony stairs, surrounded by admiring females. I couldn't help but wonder if someone who looked that good could also dance, since I loved ballroom and jitterbug dancing. You could call it infatuation at first sight. Ev told me later, "I just knew Don was the one you'd pick for yourself."

I managed an introduction, although we had to push past several females to do so. To my pleasant surprise, "Don" proved to be a superb dancer. He later asked me if I would join him at an after-hours night spot. What I didn't know was that he was quite a drinker and, in the course of the evening, he forgot that he had asked me out. When Jackson's closed, I reminded him of our date. He was apologetic and off we went. We had only gotten as far as the front seat of his car, however, when he made a pass at me. After firmly dissuading him, he apologized and, from then on, he was a perfect gentleman. Once at the club, we had one dance, after which we were interrupted by numerous women. He seemed to have forgotten we were together, so I decided to leave. Although I was in back of him, and thought I was unnoticed, his long arm reached out behind him as I turned to go and he pulled me back. We were inseparable after that and he even made a successful effort to remain sober during the remainder of my stay.

We occasionally wrote to each other during the ensuing year. When vacation time came around again, I wrote to tell Don how much I was looking forward to seeing him. He unexpectedly replied that he was now engaged and, although he could not meet me at the airport, he would send a nice guy in his stead. I was disappointed, but not enough to cancel my vacation. However, when I arrived at the airport, there was Don waiting for me. He not only drove me to Ocean City, he spent every moment with me. There was a dynamic attraction between us, but he had his life and I had mine. I learned after I returned to Michigan that his fiancee, a redhead whom I was told resembled me, returned his ring when she found out about us. They eventually got back together and later married. Long distance romances don't stand much of a chance. Still, I often reminisce about those beautiful times.

During later years, I enjoyed Ocean City vacations with my husband and son. I wanted Todd to feel the joy of that place as I had. Years later, he and his girlfriend visited the same beach. Still later, Todd escorted me there, agreeing that it was indeed a special place. Several close friends recently took me back for a birthday celebration and a spiritual reunion of sorts. Standing on the main corner of those old stomping grounds, I felt I had a connection with a past that transcended this lifetime.

It has been fun reviewing old letters, cards, and photographs. One of my biggest laughs came during the reading of letters from various boyfriends in which they expressed that they would "love me till they die." Some of them probably don't even remember who I am. But there are some who I hope still hold very fond memories. They, too, would get a good laugh out of the letters and the youthful exuberance that accompanied them.

5
New York, New York

Kindness is the only service that withstands the storm of life and will not wash out. It will wear well, look well, and be remembered long after the prism of politeness or the complexion of courtesy has faded away.
—Abraham Lincoln

After I graduated from high school, I was accepted as a candidate for the Powers modeling school in New York City. The night before leaving, I had coffee with my friend Evelyn and she decided to join me in New York. That was the beginning of an exciting time of my life. Somehow, modeling school went by the wayside. Although Ev and I experienced difficulty finding apartments during wartime, we finally located a lovely, inexpensive Riverside Drive apartment, complete with bedbugs. While working at Radio City Music Hall in very public positions, it was humiliating for me to appear at work with one side of my face swollen from bed bug bites. I, of course, wanted to move, but Ev didn't since the bugs didn't bother her.

The two of us had rather selective jobs as uniformed service staff at Radio City, handing out programs and running the elevators. Mind you, they were gold push-button. No particular talent was required. One interesting facet of the job was to run the executive elevator – the one that carried the VIPs to the top-floor offices. We operators were taught that the president's pet peeve was for anyone to put their cosmetics in the gold executive elevator telephone box. Feeling that the box door was secure enough not to matter, yours truly had it well supplied. One day, a man got on the elevator going to the executive office and while on our way up, the phone box sprung open and all my stuff fell out. As the gentleman helped me pick up my things and reload the box, he pleasantly observed, "You must be new here." When I returned to the main floor and told about my mishap, one of the staff asked, "Do you know who that was? The president of Radio City." Good grief! I immediately thought of our explicit instructions and the nice man helping me.

While at Radio City, an unexpected opportunity arose. I was offered a chance to try out for the Rockettes chorus line. I was naturally honored and intrigued by the prospect. But then I realized that even though the dancers only worked three weeks per month, at high pay, those three weeks were nonstop rehearsals and shows. They really earned their week off. I reluctantly declined the offer. Later that year, I also turned down the chance to be a receptionist in the recording room at NBC. At eighteen, I was more concerned with money, not the contacts I could make. Live and learn.

One day on the way to work, Ev and I noticed that Frank Sinatra was appearing at the Paramount Theater. If we skipped work, we could see him. So we did. It was worth it, maybe not to Radio City, but to us. We sighed along with all the others in the audience. No question about it: Sinatra had something special.

That brings to mind my very own "Franky." His actual name was Vinny. He was in the Navy; he was young, handsome, and an outstanding vocalist. Ev was engaged to Hal, a sax player at the Aquarium nightclub on Broadway. Vinny was often a guest vocalist there. The women were mad about him. When he sang, they swooned and I joined them. After convincing Hal to introduce me to Vinny, he asked me to dance. Talk about being on Cloud Nine.

When Vinny later left the club, it felt as though my heart had gone with him. Everyone warned me not to get too attached because he never entered there or left with anyone. A few moments later, he returned to the club and asked me to dance with him again. He said when he left the club, he just couldn't forget me; that I was very sweet. In a high-powered place like New York City, I guess Ev and I did stand out as being wholesomely different.

That was the beginning of a romance that really touched my life. Imagine how proud I felt when Vinny would be asked to sing while he was dancing with me. He would get on stage, hold my hand, and sing directly to me: songs like "The More I See You," "What a Difference a Day Makes" and "I'll Be Seeing You." When walking arm-in-arm along Broadway at night after the club closed, Vinny would sing to me alone. For me, he made the words come to life. I regretfully lost touch with him after he returned to duty and I returned home. I didn't learn until much later that when he was next in port, another sailor with whom I was barely acquainted told Vinny he was my "husband" (complete with "children" at home). What was *supposed* to be a joke was definitely not funny to me and most likely a real surprise to Vinny. What a sad ending to a beautiful time.

Approaching Christmas of that year, Ev and I took extended leaves from Radio City, thus giving up our jobs. When I arrived home, I really was very puffed up – thought I was pretty much *it*, and that my hometown was old hat. When I had moved to New York City, I was happy to be leaving a place where everyone, but everyone, knew me. It had been fun to be on my own in New York, only to run into unexpected reminders of Ann Arbor, including the mayor's son, the owners of a local store, plus a high school friend serving in the Navy. Now, back home at holiday time, it was kind of fun to run into people I knew. I guess I was more homesick than I had realized.

Over the Christmas holidays, my brother introduced me to Johnny, a friend of his who was ten years my senior, divorced, and with a young daughter back home in Kentucky. It was still wartime, and Ford Motor Company had brought him to Michigan to run "center wing" of the bomber plant at Willow Run Airport, east of town. Being new to the area and knowing few people, Johnny asked me if I would go out with him on New Year's Eve. I automatically said no, feeling I didn't know him well enough, he was too old for me, etc. But as he started to drive away, I hollered out the window (no time for niceties) that I'd changed my mind and to pick me up later. He did and that was the beginning of a surprising romance – and definitely a good-bye to New York City.

I really had no romantic interest in Johnny at first. When he told me that within three weeks, I would be in love with him, I had quite a laugh. But in three weeks, I was totally in love. In fact, Johnny was one of the great loves of my life. He was wise but down-to-earth and a great tease. When people would peek in his office asking for "Mr. V" (Johnny), he'd tell them, "He's out. I'm Johnny."

At that time, I was a secretary to the head of Labor Relations at the bomber plant. Johnny's office was about a mile away within the plant. One day, someone from his office came up to me with a message from him that I could not ride to work with him anymore. I marched straight to his office, only to find him sitting with his feet propped on his desk, laughing his head off. He said, "I wondered just how long it would take you to get down here." He well knew I wouldn't take such news lightly.

In the spring of that year, Ford Motor called Johnny back to Louisville where he became head of a major division. He loved me, but when discussing anything serious, he said he would come back in a few months to see if I really knew what I wanted. He tried to sneak away without saying good-bye on that last morning. I awoke and ran sobbing to the driveway, only to discover that he was crying, too.

By June, I had met Tom. He was just out of the paratroopers, good-looking and sweet, kind of bashful. All thoughts of Johnny temporarily aside, I was attracted to this Gregory Peck look-alike and we began dating. I had already arranged for a summer job as secretary to a businessman who owned much of Mackinac Island. I managed to get Tom, his friend Jack, and my friend Arlene jobs at the Island, too. By summer's end, I had fallen for Tom. Yet one evening, I could talk of nothing but Johnny. Tom must have wondered what was wrong with me: cold feet, second thoughts? The next morning, I got a call from Mom: "Guess who was here last night and tried to call you?" It was Johnny, who kept his word about coming back to see if I knew what I really wanted. I thought I did.

Tom and I dated for another year, after which we were married. Our twenty-some years together consisted of fairly ordinary and busy times: making a home for ourselves and our son; attending PTA meetings and Little League games; pursuing our careers; entertaining friends and relatives; sandwiching in occasional golf, bowling, stage shows and movies; and enjoying our companion animals – all the things most American families do. But, as in many relationships, our differences ultimately led to the breakdown of our life as a couple. Although it's obvious I've always had a life, married and otherwise, it just becomes even more meaningful as it progresses.

Photographs

Little Doris in practice for things to come.

"You say you want to help animals?"
(Might even become a member.)

"And Mr. Amory told you to call me?'
(It must be serious.)

"Don't worry. I'll protect you," Doris assures Buddy.

Young Doris and friend.

Photographs

There's something about a uniform . . .

"Juniors on Parade."

The Grand Finale.
Doris is seventh from the right.

Friends – Doris and Arlene on Detroit to Mackinac Yacht Race Winner.
(Below) "Redhead" and Red Boy.

Doris in Radio City staff uniform.

Photographs

Doris and Evelyn with members of the Eighth Army Air Corps.

"Marlon, Jr."

Doris' favorite sailor . . .
until "Franky."

My "Franky."

Mark's Dad.

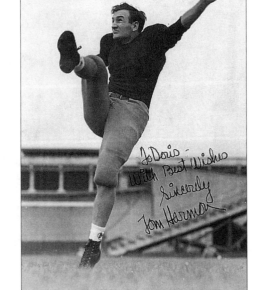

Photographs

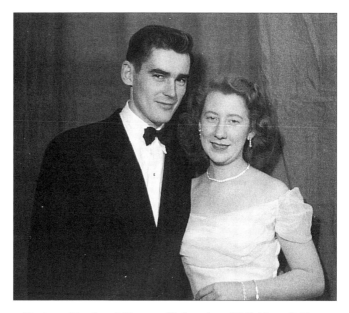

Doris and husband, Tom, at University of Michigan J-Hop.

Todd returning from Hawaii to Michigan winter.

PooKoo's sentiments to animal dealers.

KoKo watching the first moon landing live on TV, featured on the cover of the *Shelter News* of the National Cat Protection Society.

Doris and Jethro.

Photographs

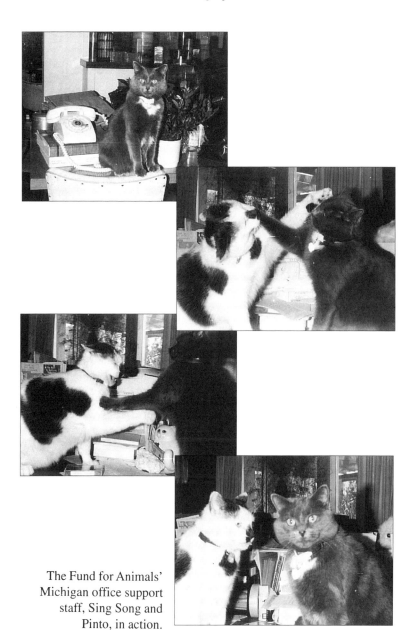

The Fund for Animals' Michigan office support staff, Sing Song and Pinto, in action.

Dear Mr. Amory,

Enclosed is one of my all-time favorite bullfighting photos. As you can see, the bull is making a social comment on the "art" of bullfighting . . . and it looks like his point is well taken!
Thank you for Fund for Animals . . . there is so much to be done. But you and F.F.A. give direction and a VOICE to many concerned people. You're great!

    –L.A. Moffitt
      Huntington Beach, CA

Blinding cruelty at the rodeo.

Chauncey's Cougar Caravan with Cleveland Amory, Doris, the Derbys, and famous sports figures.

Photographs

From left, Doris Dixon, Doris Day, Cleveland Amory, and Cindy Traisi, author of *Because They Matter*.

DORIS DAY

Dear Doris,   February 14, 1986

How nice it was to hear from an old friend, and I'm pleased to know that you still head the Michigan Office of The Fund for Animals. I'm happy that you like my show. It was great having Cleveland on, and I think that was one of the best segments so far. He came back to Carmel a few weeks ago to do an interview with me for *Parade*.

I loved all the clippings you enclosed and the articles you wrote. They were excellent. By the way, I think it's great that you taught a class on Animal Rights at the college. Wouldn't it be great if that were offered at every college or even in high schools? Education is so important to humane work. Most people know nothing about animal welfare.

Thanks again for writing, Doris. I loved hearing from you. Keep up the good work!

Thanks for caring!
Doris

P.S. I thought you might enjoy seeing a couple of our recent newsletters from The Doris Day Pet Foundation, so I'll enclose them.

Never mind the smile – if you collect fur coats, steer clear of Doris Dixon

A former private eye, this Ann Arbor woman is an army of one, hell bent on animals rights.

In the tumble of history, protection of the animals that share (or formerly shared) our globe has frequently fallen by default into the wrong hands.

John J. Audubon, for example, may have inspired a national bird-protection society, but he still got his kicks by shooting the smithereens out of the winged creatures he so artfully illustrated. Bull-Mooser Teddy Roosevelt spoke softly for conservation, but carried a big elephant gun. And in our own era, England's Prince Philip scores environmental consciousness points by serving as a high mucky-muck in the World Wildlife Fund, but big-game hunting remains his idea of jolly good fun.

Most of the rest of us are divided, animal-wise, into two categories. We are either (A) hunters with varying degrees of commitment to conservation, or (B) non-hunters who tsk-tsk at television exposes of animal cruelty, but will probably go through life never realizing that Buffalo Bill was a slaughter-crazy nerd.

Ask any bear if he can count on either Category A or B for the survival of himself and his descendants and he will probably collapse with laughter into the nearest honeycomb. What he might tell you, however, is that his survival and that of his animal brethren – if, indeed, they do survive – will probably be the result of a lot of hard work by a relative handful of people who are occasionally ridiculed and almost never remembered with granite monuments after they have slipped these earthly bonds.

People like Ann Arbor's Doris Dixon.

Portion of article by Tom Hennessy in the Sunday Magazine
Section of the *Detroit Free Press*, August 29, 1976.

6
All God's Creatures

If you have men who will exclude any of God's creatures from the shelter of pity and compassion, you will have men who will deal likewise with their fellow men.
—St. Francis of Assisi

To most of us, compassion comes in all shapes and sizes. We believe it should be rightfully extended to all creatures, not just the endangered or photogenic ones. Just because an animal is different from us doesn't mean she or he isn't deserving of our respect. I dedicate the following poem to all living creatures.

Of Life
I nearly killed you! . . . but then I thought
Why? Just because I can?
Just because you look different than I –

(you've done me no harm).
Just because I am unable to understand
your way of life –
Just because I have not stopped to think
that a force greater than either of us
caused you to be here for a purpose
and very possibly a purpose as important as mine?
Just because someone led me to believe it was acceptable?
(I really need not do it to survive).
Who knows – we might be the best of friends
if only I realized the truth.
So . . . Now you live, and I am glad you live.
I feel better for it than had I ended,
or even hindered, Your Life.
And I say, welcome to my part of the world.
I'll do my best to make your stay pleasant
until I know a better way to help you
along your journey on earth, as a wiser mentor intended.

That poem went to the printer and when I picked up the copies later, the lady behind the desk said, "Oh, you wrote that. It's very interesting – I was sitting out in the yard this weekend after reading that and there were some ants crawling on my hand. My impulse is always just to kill them, but now I realized I was sitting on their house."

Many in the animal cause find that, perhaps because of their empathy with all living things, they are acutely aware of the interconnectedness of all life. I have had many experiences that made me a believer.

When my sassamutt PooKoo died, the local humane society sent me their formal condolence card. On the front was a familiar-looking face: a sketch of *PooKoo* herself (although the humane society didn't realize it), drawn by Michigan artist and family friend, Bill Shurtliff. The sketch had been done in PooKoo's younger days and had found its way onto the humane society's stationery, and hence to me.

Like PooKoo, a similar thread in the web of our life was our Siamese, KoKo. He was exceptional: soft, brown, and creamy, with blue eyes, white whiskers, and a practically nonstop purr. If every friend were as fair and loyal, the world would be a much nicer place. Training was not much of a problem: he had us all trained within six months! Every evening, I would go from my kitchen and living room downstairs to the bath and bedroom upstairs several times. Though always near my side, the only time KoKo would join me on the upward leg of my journey was on my last trip for the evening, when I was ready for bed. At first, I thought it was because I made some particular moves that indicated it was the last trip upstairs for the night. Not so. I checked and rechecked by changing any particular cue he might perceive, such as leaving on or turning out certain lights. I finally realized he had the ability to comprehend my intentions. People who don't understand animals don't know how much they're missing.

Two years after KoKo's death, I received a copy of the *Shelter News* of the National Cat Protection Society in California. On the cover was a picture of KoKo. I contacted them and found that they didn't know how the picture had come into their possession. I explained that when the astronauts first landed on the moon in 1969, I had been watching television with my family and had KoKo on my lap when a friend took a picture of us. Somehow the photograph found its way to its rightful place in the scheme of things. I told them I was happy to see KoKo still carrying on his work – *his* way! He continues to work his magic on my life as well, prompting me to dedicate this poem to him:

Of Love
You came to me last night in a moonbeam.
Although I could not see you in the usual ways
I knew you were here.
As yesterday, today or tomorrow, you will be
with me in so many ways – a droplet of water,
a ray of sun, a whisper of the wind,
the green of grass, a leaf, a tree, a melody,
in the air I breathe.
Thank you for sharing my life.
You still make light the heavier times
bringing a brightness to that which is dim.
Your spirit and warmth are forever.
I love you, my soulmate.
You always let me know what it is to be
appreciated – by being with me.

It is often said that mighty things come in small packages. A black fluff of a kitten, Midnight Snowball was found by Todd when she was about ten weeks old, playing in the middle of traffic downtown. After exhausting all efforts to locate her original home, we came to the conclusion that we were to be her family. As Todd so aptly put it, "Mom, we can't turn her over to anyone else, because we understand animals and no one else would put up with her." She was *that* kind of a cat – into everything she wished. During her first week with us, she managed to spread white flour all over her black fur. And food from a trash bag was always *much* more appetizing than anything in her dish. Then there was that favorite habit of sleeping in my lingerie drawer with so many things to rearrange while preparing her bed. Chasing bubbles in the outdoor waterbed was another wonderful (summer) pastime. Mind you, she wasn't nearly all bad (even though after three adoring strokes from someone, she would swat them to indicate that was the limit). Now she has gone to join KoKo and PooKoo, both of whom adored her, as did we, sometimes at a safe distance, depending upon her mood. I believe we have much to learn from animals and Snowby was here as both a teacher and a friend.

While holding a regular job as a secretary at Washtenaw Community College in order to make ends meet (whoever said animal rights people don't have a life – or two!), I met Pinto, another of my animal mentors. He came up from the basement of the old building that housed our office. He was a scroungy, beat-up looking cat, but he soon warmed up to a kind voice and good food. After receiving veterinary care and neutering, he returned to my office. While waiting for someone to claim him, he disappeared. Visions of traps and training bait for dogfights crowded my mind. Three weeks later, the morning after Easter, he inexplicably appeared from behind the basement door and thereafter served as the honorary office cat. Nearly a year later, when I left the office for the day, I closed Pinto once again in his loft off my office, with food and access to the nearby woods. I gave him his usual pat and admonished him, "Goodnight. Be a good boy. Have fun and I'll see you tomorrow." Well, tomorrow he was not there, nor was he ever there again. I prayed, "A year and a half with him wasn't really enough – with the exception that it was long enough for a deep love to set in – a love that makes me miss him terribly. Couldn't I just have him a while longer? If he is with you, God, please let me know. If he is not, please let me have him back." Four months later, I received a call from my friend, Dee Gibson Strom, who worked at the local humane society. She told me Pinto was there. I dashed out, heart thumping. It was, indeed, Pinto. After a day and a night at the vet's, he came home with me: a miracle and a blessing I cannot adequately describe.

And then there was Sing Song, again from the woods on the college grounds. Whatever had scared this feline twenty feet up into a pine tree for the night, she responded to my call, realizing that I had given her food and kindness the day before. A treasure not to be left behind, she became a member of our home family. How do I describe such a wonderful gray four-pawed being? She was a favorite of everyone – always in attendance at the door and all gatherings, and always being her sweet, though sometimes mischievous, self. I often referred to her as Houdini, as she could open any door that was not tightly secured. When she joined that world beyond in her mid-teens, we lost an Angel on Earth. She had opened the door to our hearts that could not be closed.

Another miracle who also came from the woods near the college was Tawny, a lost and bloody-pawed cat who, despite all she'd undoubtedly been through, was extremely affectionate. She showed up in my office on the first day of classes and immediately jumped onto my desk and from there, onto my lap. This particular behavior made my decision to adopt her even easier, for although I already had three very affectionate cats at home, none were "lap cats." Her ploy certainly worked and although she would thereafter snuggle close by me, she *never* again sat on my lap. She was a con artist supreme, and an ever-loving one, at that.

Those woods were a magical place, from which emerged yet another of my feline companions. Bobbi was truly a wild thing. She lived in and around my college office for five years while I cared for her as much as she would permit me to. Not wanting to leave her behind when I retired from the college, I attempted to livetrap her. After *three* attempts, and some ingenuity (on my part), I finally outwitted her (or, more likely, she decided to let me win for once). Bobbi was truly street smart and, as I liked to tease, a "phantom cat," for no one but myself usually saw her. After capturing her, it took *three* vets to successfully anesthetize her before giving her medical treatment (shots, spaying, etc.). I told them to give her anything she would ever need because they'd never see her again; nor have they, true to her phantom reputation.

After the vet stay, I brought Bobbi home and released her in my den. She was *not* a happy cat. After hiding from Todd and me in a crawlspace and then under a sofa, we decided to take a chance and leave the den door open. It took Bobbi very little time to get the run of the house, and to be accepted by our other cats, whom she had probably hung out with when they had all lived in the woods near the college. The next day, however, we couldn't find Bobbi anywhere. We searched the house, afraid she'd somehow escaped. One of my friends who rehabilitates and cares for feral cats advised me not to worry. She assured me Bobbi had found a hiding place and that she would come out when she was ready and would then show me her safe spot. A short time later, while I was feeding the other cats, Bobbi suddenly joined them. After eating, she led us to two spots in our basement (in the rafters and under the stairwell) as if to say, "Don't worry about me." She would thereafter often leave her hiding places and even sleep on my bed.

To make life easier for the still somewhat wild Bobbi and the others, we decided to build an enclosed outdoor area for their comfort. This sanctuary featured a 6' x 10' x 6' fenced enclosure, with access to the indoors. It included junipers, a burning bush, a tree trunk for scratching, a grassy patch and even a concrete slab to roll on. From this haven, the cats, especially Bobbi, could watch the wildlife, but not harm them, or cause harm to themselves by running into the street. We could all use such a sanctuary from time to time to recuperate in safety from our battle scars. As for Bobbi, her story continues and would require another book to fully do her justice.

7
Special Friends

I would not enter on my list of friends (though graced with polished manners and fine sense) the man who needlessly sets foot upon a worm.
–WIlliam Cowper

When Todd was fourteen, he and I were fortunate enough to share a learning experience and friendship with Carl Marty of Northernaire in Three Lakes, Wisconsin. Northernaire was a sanctuary for wildlife as well as a popular resort visited by politicians and celebrities alike. Bob Hope was one of Northernaire's most notable visitors. Sterling North, author of *Rascal*, *Raccoons are the Brightest People*, and *Wolfling*, among others, once observed, "In America's last century and a half, there have been three great naturalists: Thoreau, Muir, and Carl Marty. I have written books about all of them and of the three, I love Carl Marty the best." Having read an article

Todd wrote on "Cruelty to Animals" for a national humane magazine, Carl invited him to spend summer vacation at his resort, rightly known as "The Waldorf of the Wilderness."

Todd helped care for a variety of orphaned animals who were returned to the wild as soon as they were able to survive on their own. Carl and his Vilas Oneidas Wilderness Society also fought against hunting and trapping of wildlife. During his stay, Todd received a plaque from them for his outstanding efforts on behalf of animals. Working in conjunction with such an outstanding humanitarian and naturalist was a great education for my son, as well as for myself.

In later years as a Fund representative, I met George, a zoologist and former vice president for a large pharmaceutical company. He asked for my help on behalf of his private organization, the Zoological Action Program. He was trying to stop Wayne State University in Detroit from using chimps in their highway crash tests. He made it clear to me that his only interest was endangered species. I agreed to help the chimps and together we managed to exert enough public pressure on the university to stop the testing.

Our ensuing friendship resulted in George becoming far more involved in animal rights than he ever expected. He became particularly aware of the abuses animals were subjected to by companies such as his employer. He would often share with me his growing disillusionment with this aspect of research.

When George retired to Florida, he faced the dilemma of what to do with a small jungle cat he had come into possession of some sixteen years earlier and who was by now a beloved member of his family. He feared she was too old to relocate and had considered euthanizing her if it was the only humane alternative. Instead, I managed to temporarily place her with friends who custom-built a large area in their basement where she could feel secure. After George and his family settled in Florida, he moved his cat down and she lived out her natural life with them. It was then that I asked him, "When you had a problem very close to you regarding a living thing, who did you come to – your scientific friends or your humane friends?" He replied that he came to me, of course. After all, it was clear that I regarded planet Earth and its inhabitants as safest in humane hands.

Among other memorable experiences was meeting Richard Bach, author of *Johnathan Livingston Seagull*. After having read his book on the advice of a friend who insisted, "This is you, Doris," I found myself strongly identifying with Jonathan's desire to achieve what looked like the impossible. At that time, there were too few people willing to stick their necks out to help animals.

While running the Chicago Fund office in the early seventies, I saw Bach on a morning TV program. I got the name of his hotel from the station and invited him to have breakfast with Cleveland and me. He did, and in him I found a kindred spirit. I asked his birthsign and after diplomatically replying "all signs," the private eye in me persisted until he admitted to being a Gemini, as am I. I, too, love flying and daring to be different. When we took our leave (after Richard agreed with Cleveland to help in our endeavors), I said most directly, "I hope we meet again." He pointed at me and said, "It will happen." To date it has not, but I have every faith it will, in one way or another. We seem to be on a very similar spiritual path, although I believe his is perhaps more advanced.

Jerry St. James, a popular San Diego area disc jockey, is a particularly close friend and strong animals rights supporter. While working at a Detroit radio station in the seventies, he contacted me to see if The Fund was an organization he wanted to join. I told him we were IT. He came over immediately and it was accomplishments from there on. One of his major achievements was the Jerry St. James/Fund for Animals "Save the Dolphins" mini-golf tournament, with thousands in attendance. National celebrities, such as Eartha Kitt, as well as local ones like Mark "The Bird" Fidrych, the hot Detroit Tiger pitcher, made appearances, as did Cleveland Amory himself.

Jerry has gone on to establish the Unicorn Foundation to, as he puts it, "speak for those who can't: the animals." Jerry continues:

> Animals provide us with companionship, offer us protection, endow us with joy, amaze us with their mystery and beauty. Our stage production, "Bless the Beasts," is designed as an educational experience for the general public, the vast numbers of people who are noticing that animals and their rights are becoming big social issues, people who know very little about the horrors experienced by so many animals, people who are manipulated by slick public relations efforts and kept purposefully "in the dark" about the crimes of animal genocide. The majority of people are really very good and decent. They will do what they can to stop injustices when they find out about them. And when people find out the truth about animals, when they get a peek behind laboratory doors and slaughterhouse walls, when they are shown the horrors of factory farming, when they learn about the fur and entertainment industries and other areas of animal abuse, when they are exposed to the folly of it all, they call for it to stop. I wish to

express my thanks to some incredible people, including Doris Dixon of the Michigan Office of The Fund for Animals. When I came to her in 1975, she began with great patience teaching me to turn my blind furor over animal abuse into civilized and positive ways to effect change. Fifteen years later, she is still showing me how it should be done.

In addition to meeting many exciting people in the animal cause, I have met some of the most unusual and wonderful animals. Little did I realize that one of the highlights of my life would be my friendship with wolves, in particular two wolves named Jethro and Clem. They came my way while they were doing educational programs with the National Association for the Preservation of Predatory Animals. Jethro had already attained celebrity status, appearing with Dick Cavett, Hugh Downs, Jim Fowler, at Carnegie Hall, and as the background howls for Paul Winter recordings. When his "person," John Harris, was asked, "How do you train a wolf?" he responded, "It's easy – you train them to do anything *they* want to do." John continually stressed that wolves are wild animals and need to be respected as such. The animals he cared for had been injured by hunters and trappers. None were bred for, or intended to be, pets or curiosity items. Together with John and his crew, the wolves traveled the country in their very own den on wheels, as their special van was called.

Cleveland asked that I arrange our Fund booth at the 1972 Chicago World Flower and Garden Show. This assignment included making lodging and publicity arrangements for Jethro and those select human celebrities who would accompany him. Panicked, I called Marian Probst to ask, "When would be the best time to break the news to Cleveland that I have never even attended a garden show? Remind him the only reason I said 'yes' was that I was too weak with the flu to say anything more complicated." But Cleveland is a hard person to say "no" to, and so I found myself spending several weeks planning an appropriate setting for Jethro at Chicago's McCormick Place, complete with pine trees and logs.

Memories of Jethro coming down the children's slide at the Holiday Inn in Chicago were a wonderful first. It took very little coaxing and the second time down was his idea! He was, indeed, the wolf ambassador and representative supreme for his fellow four-footed kind. Visitors at the show included Chicago Mayor Richard Daley as well as Illinois Governor and Mrs. Ogilvie. Later that same year, Governor Ogilvie signed into law the Endangered Species Act for Illinois. We feel certain that his personal meeting with Jethro had an impact on this endeavor. Everyone agreed that the highlight of the show was the presentation of the "Animal of the Year Award" from Cleveland to Jethro. It read, "For Jethro – wolf without peer and animal extraordinaire. An ambassador without portfolio or collar – who has traveled the country from coast to coast, with patience, understanding, and fortitude, to plead the cause of all animals everywhere." Jethro graciously accepted it with a nibble on the corner.

Later, during an appearance on the televised *Bob Cromie Show* in Chicago, Jethro seemed to enjoy his celebrity status. But when he decided it was time to end the show, he proceeded to take the whole set off the stage by pulling at the rug underneath. No question who upstaged all on that production.

In the ensuing two years, I was privileged to have Jethro, Clem, and their people as my guests. My outstanding memories of Jethro and Clem are of their beautiful howls at night and in the early morning, while resting among the trees in my yard. Even my dogs enjoyed a romp with them. I could tell that, upon our third meeting, Jethro was accepting me as a pack member. Being the alpha wolf, it was imperative that pack members come to him before addressing any other wolves. I noticed that if I went to Clem first, Jethro would properly scold me; he knew that I finally realized the difference.

Three incidents come to mind regarding Jethro and Clem's many educational appearances in Michigan and Canada. One was a visit on the late J.P. McCarthy's *Focus*, a show on WJR radio in Detroit. J.P. had met everyone who was anyone, but seemed quite relieved that Jethro decided to sleep on the other side of the room during the interview rather than actively participating. During Jethro's appearance on the WXYZ-TV *Morning Show* in Detroit, Rosey Greer was also a guest. Although a bit apprehensive at first, at breakfast after the show, he admitted that he really thought Jethro was OK. ("I wouldn't even mind having one live next door to me.") Last but not least was the great kinship shown by Bill Grosscup of *Woods and Wheels*, a popular Canadian outdoors television program. Because of his enthusiasm for The Fund, as well as for John Harris and his work, Bill invited John and the wolves to make an appearance at the Detroit Sportsmen's Conference, where they brought to light some truths about wolves and why it is not "sport" to kill them.

Besides the many schools and museums we visited, I also had the pleasure of scheduling Jethro and Clem's appearance on the *Phil Donahue Show* with Cleveland. In my initial correspondence with the show's producer, I teased, "Are you ready for the most exciting thing yet – something really special for your audience? With these wolves, their guardians, and Cleveland, I guarantee you will have a fantastic show. Quite honestly, the wolves are more predictable than Cleveland. You may tell him I said so. I'll try to see that they are properly fed prior to the appearance so that they do not devour your furniture. Jethro liked his 'Animal of the Year Award' so much that he ate it (well, not quite; just a 'token of thanks' nibble)." That appearance went off as planned and the wolves scored yet another victory in enlightening the public to the cause of their species.

In 1973, Jethro and Clem were found dead in their van, poisoned by a deranged woman who claimed to hate dogs. The case went to court and the judge found her not guilty, arguing that the wolves were at best worth only the cost of their pelts. I could only lament in my letter to the *Ann Arbor News*, "Today, your friends and mine, Jethro and Clem, are gone. Once more, humankind proves its ignorant viciousness. It would almost seem the lessons we have tried so hard to teach are for naught. May I be wrong so that others may grow up in a world with more hope of decency."

Another of my animal compatriots was Chauncey, the Lincoln-Mercury ad cougar. He had been a crippled zoo "reject" who had been taken in by Pat and Ted Derby of Love Is An Animal, an organization which rehabilitated animals formerly used in zoos or in the entertainment industry. A Lincoln-Mercury spokesman explained Chauncey's distinctiveness. "Although he never growled about his troubled early life, a birth defect played a major role in shaping the famous tough-cat image. Because of a deformed hip, the cat had to be taught to walk by the Derbys. Unable to spring like other cougars, Chauncey affected a menacing snarl as a defense mechanism. It was to make him famous. He would snarl as part of a big bluff."

When I finally had the opportunity to meet Chauncey, I

was so taken by his gentleness and his magnificence that all I could think of was how his kind was brutalized, poisoned, hunted, and trapped – and all of this suffering for what? If more humans were, in general, just half as decent as animals, what a better world we would have.

As part of a fundraising effort on behalf of animals, the Derbys and Chauncey toured the United States in a large airconditioned van, carrying both the cat and a new Cougar XR7. The car was autographed en route by such notables as Jimmy Stewart, Lucille Ball, Ed Asner, James Coburn, Valerie Harper, Charlton Heston, Leonard Nimoy, Debbie Reynolds, Henry Ford II, Muhammad Ali, Joe Frazier, Gordie Howe, Stan Musial, Al Kaline, Jesse Owens, and many others. The car was later auctioned at the Detroit Auto Show, with proceeds going to The Fund for Animals and Love Is An Animal. It was my pleasure to deliver the keys to the winning bidder in Chicago.

8
As the Twig Is Bent, So Grows the Tree

Teaching a child not to step on a caterpillar is as valuable to the child as it is to the caterpillar.
—Bradley Miller

    The greatest blessing of my marriage is my son, Todd, who is a godsend for both me and the planet's animals. He was my conscience and critic even when he was a kid, helping me realize the cruelties of rodeo and the like. He has always stood up for his beliefs, whether it be as a letter writer supreme on animal issues or by pitching in and helping with a myriad of Fund tasks and animal rescues.

    When Todd was six, I proudly decorated his bedroom wall with a wolf skin I had purchased at a local shop. It *seemed* to make sense at the time, since we both loved animals. When I became involved in the animal cause, I realized how ironic it was for anyone who loves animals to exhibit them much as a trophy-hunter might. He agreed and asked me what we should do with the wolf skin. I decided to leave it up as a symbol of my former ignorance. It later deteriorated so badly that we threw it away. It was a sad yet powerful learning experience.

For many years, Todd had intervals of wanderlust that took him throughout Canada and the United States and to a sailing school that covered much of the Caribbean. He also visited Europe, Morocco, Hong Kong, Macau, and Tahiti. Over the years, he has told me, "It's endless. No matter how much you travel, you can never see all there is." I think this conclusion led him in recent years to slow down a bit and focus more on helping nonhuman animals and those of us who care about them. He is my right-hand man and one of my strongest supporters.

When he was very young, I used to occasionally take him to rodeos. He'd ask, "Mom, isn't that cruel?" I'd reply, "No, it *couldn't* be or they wouldn't allow it." That's what I believed at the time. He would continue to argue, "You can't tell me it isn't cruel to slam those calves on the ground like that." And I thought, well, my son isn't stupid. I'm going to take a harder look into this. As I did, I realized he was right. Those animals don't volunteer to go into the arena.

Rodeo is big business, with annual prize money totaling in the millions of dollars. It is not surprising that, under such circumstances, rodeo participants are more often semiprofessional ath-

Drawing by Ashleigh Brilliant.

letes than ranchhands. Some are drawn to the "sport" because, as one observer put it, "They're too lazy to work, too nervous to steal, and too jealous to pimp."

Although rodeo is touted as an "American tradition" and "good family fun," it is condemned by every major animal protection organization in the United States. It presents countless dangers to the animals. They may be badly bruised while trapped in the chute or suffer muscle and tendon injuries while bucking, charging or being roped and dragged. They are often shocked out of the chute with an electric prod, while a flank strap is used on broncos and bulls to insure they will buck. This strap is tightened around the animal's groin, pressing on vital nerves. The more the animal writhes and bucks to rid itself of the pain, the more the strap rubs.

Most rodeo animals are actually farm animals who are owned by livestock contractors. They, in turn, lease the animals for repeated rodeo abuse. That is why flank straps and other painful methods must be used to encourage wild behavior. A veterinarian isn't required to be present at a rodeo and injured or sick animals seldom, if ever, receive medical attention. From beginning to end, there is no "sport" in rodeo.

One animal-cruelty investigator, Robert DeWolfe, described his experiences with rodeos in a letter to a Michigan state representative. "For twenty-eight years, I worked as a humane law enforcement officer and monitored countless rodeos. Never once did I encounter anyone from the Michigan Department of Agriculture or the State Veterinarian's Office. As one smashed cowhand told me at the State Fairgrounds in Detroit: 'F—you, cop, get lost! How the hell can you have a rodeo without cruelty!' It was perilous to make an arrest, but make them I did; just like it is today, the judiciary was mostly indifferent to the suffering of nonhumans and the punishment (if any) was light and ineffective. I know rodeo intimately and I know it to be cruel, ruthless, crass, insensitive and indifferent – animal mistreatment for a fast buck. Rodeo is NOT a heritage from the Old West that we should perpetuate, unless we include slavery, burning at the stake those suspected of witchcraft, and the branding of promiscuous women."

In spite of the obvious cruelties, there are even rodeos for youngsters, where, in an apparent effort to build future rodeo audiences, children are encouraged to chase calves, lambs, and other young animals. Our children receive a mixed message when on one hand, they are urged by society to be kind to animals and on the other hand, they see animals routinely terrorized in socially-sanctioned "entertainment."

In a society as rife with violence as ours, we should be encouraging kindness instead of bringing up our youth on the excitement of the chase and the kill. Certainly a person displays true strength when he or she is *helping* animals, not hurting them.

It is a well-documented fact that many criminals, including serial killers such as Jeffrey Dahmer, tortured and killed animals when they were children. As retired Ann Arbor police detective George Stauch once told me during an interview, "I have noticed that children who were kind and considerate to their pets were rarely involved in any matters that necessitated police action, even later in adult years. Children who were abusive to animals usually had little concern for their playmates. Most of these children in later years became a problem to society. They had little concern for authority or the rights of others."

> **Lack of humane education
> is the principal cause of crime.**
> –Journal of Education

Despite the great number of animal abuses that society tolerates and even condones, I believe that *education* is the key to change. Most people wouldn't be indulging in these abuses if they realized what was actually going on. Like so many social and moral causes, there's a long way to go; but we've come a long way!

Washtenaw Community College (WCC) was one of the first institutions in the country to offer "Introduction to the Humane Movement/Animal Rights," which I taught. My seminar has since served as a model for similar classes elsewhere. I was encouraged in this endeavor by WCC's music director and jazz great, the late Morris Lawrence. He had always been a strong supporter of mine, good-naturedly referring to me as "Mother Nature." With enthusiasm from both faculty and students, the class was so well-received that I taught several more seminars before turning to other priorities of the animal cause. Each year, I host students from an area high school's Social Science class. I answer their questions and supply them with information on a wide variety of animal issues. Below are excerpts from a few of the many thank you letters I have received:

> We all appreciate your continued support of the Social Action Projects. You've reached seven hundred kids by doing this. In addition, they talk to family and friends so the word is really getting out! Thanks for your "life work" and thanks for being so good to us!

> We appreciate you letting us come over to your house and learn from you and your experiences with The Fund for Animals.

We learned a lot and had fun at the animal rights rally.

I'd like to be a strong part of The Fund for Animals. I've learned so much and I'd really like to be seriously involved. I feel great about the wildlife workshop, but there's so much more that needs to be done. I'll feel really great when it's all abolished. I hope our presentations drew a lot of people towards joining and acting. We really put our hearts, minds, and feelings into it and I believe we represented them well. We surely touched a lot of people, but I'd like to see some action.

It really was an excellent experience going to the candlelight protest for National Lab Animal Day. There really are a lot of willing people. After doing this, I'm much more aware and look at things a lot differently.

I would like to thank you for the time and effort that you have put aside just to pass on your knowledge to us younger generations, showing us to care. It is people like you that make a difference.

You personally made me stop and think about the many emotional and physical needs animals live for. I have learned so many heartbreaking things. It helped me educate two whole hours of classes. Everyone was touched, heartbroken, tearful, and concerned.

It made me happy to see that you treated us as adults and answered our questions to the best of your knowledge. We learned a lot.

In addition, I was pleased to be honored on Martin Luther King Day in 1993 by Carrie Smith, an elementary school student as the "one person she knows who shares something important with Dr. King's work, beliefs, and his dream." Carrie wrote:

> The person who most reminds me of Martin Luther King, Jr. is my friend Doris Dixon. She is like Dr. King because she stands up for her beliefs, no matter what the cost. For over twenty-five years, Doris has worked with The Fund for Animals. The Fund is made up of people from all around the world who are united in their belief that animals have rights, too. They believe that animals should not be harmed. Doris was one of the first people to work for The Fund. She was chosen by Cleveland Amory, founder of The Fund. Doris is in charge of its Michigan office. She has many responsibilities, such as investigating cases of cruelty to animals, working to pass laws that will help animals, teaching classes on animal rights, organizing volunteers to protest hunting, furs, animal experimentation, rodeos, etc. I helped Doris with The Fund for Animals booth at the Art Fair last year. I got to talk to many people who believe as we do and to try to convince other people why it is wrong to hurt animals. I think Doris Dixon is a great person. I really look up to her. She has taught me to never give up on something you believe in. The animals really need all our help. So if you

want to make this world a better place for people and animals, please think about joining The Fund or at least helping in your own way. Thank you.

Many of the students and other volunteers I work with often say, "Oh, I could never do what you've done." I remind them that they've *already* done more than I had at their age and they're here with me to learn. No one knows what they're capable of until they try. I've never done anything that any of them can't do. *All it takes is a lot of caring and a little daring.* Many of my volunteers have gone on to outstanding accomplishments: forming new coalitions, addressing new issues, breathing new life into an ever-growing movement

Because the road to humaneness is a long one, three ingredients for success are essential: *desire, determination, and dedication.* The advice of those who have proven their staying power can be invaluable, to both you and the animals. No matter how insignificant you may at times feel, *everything* you do makes a difference! Each of us, acting alone, may not feel we have much of an impact on society. But when joined with others of like mind and determination, our achievements can be astonishing. Remember, it takes at least *three* exposures to a new idea for someone to get the point. So, whether you are the first one to approach a person or the second, you are as responsible for any ultimate change in their thinking as the third person, for you have paved the way for their receptiveness. One of my favorite poems is aptly titled *Don't Quit.*

> When things go wrong, as they sometimes will,
> When the road you're trudging seems all uphill,
> When the funds are low and the debts are high,
> And you want to smile, but you have to sigh,

When care is pressing you down a bit,
Rest if you must, but don't you quit.
Life is queer with its twists and turns,
As every one of us sometimes learns.
And many a fellow turns about
When he might have won had he stuck it out.
Don't give up though the pace seems slow,
You may succeed with another blow.
Often the goal is nearer than
It seems to a faint and faltering man;
Often the struggler has given up
When he might have captured the victor's cup.
And he learned too late when the night came down,
How close he was to the golden crown.
Success is failure turned inside out,
The silver tint of the clouds of doubt,
And you never can tell how close you are,
It may be near when it seems afar;
So stick to the fight when you're hardest hit,
It's when things seem worst that you mustn't quit.
                                        –Author unknown

There are many people who have combined their support of animals with their family lives and daily accomplishments. One such person is my friend Wanda Nash who, in addition to her years of work in the humane movement, raised a family and became an attorney at age 43. She spent a number of years as a legislative aide, an assistant prosecutor, and a private attorney dealing with child abuse and neglect cases. She formed the nonprofit Michigan Attorneys for Animals in 1992. It is now recognized by the Michigan Bar Association (for which it chartered the Animal Law Section in 1995). It is amazing what realization and dedication can accomplish.

9
A Hunting and Trapping They Will Go

When a man wantonly destroys the works of men, we call him a vandal. When he wantonly destroys the works of God we call him a sportsman.
–Joseph Wood Krutch

Until the publishing of Cleveland Amory's book, *Mankind? Our Incredible War on Wildlife* in the mid-seventies, the public was largely under the impression that the environment was being managed for the benefit of both people and animals. Well-hidden by outdoor writers and television programs was the carnage that went on behind the scenes. Outdoor programs showed famous sports or movie stars shooting at anything with four legs or two wings under the guise of sport. The victim would fall, but the camera never showed the prolonged suffering, only glib chitchat and handshaking between the guest hunter and his media host.

At one time in my life, I, too, was a product of the misguided notion that all was well in our woods. Hunters and conservation departments argued that deer and other *game* species had to be hunted to save them from starvation, with no mention of how their numbers are managed (i.e. *increased*) by state and national government wildlife agencies to satisfy the bloodthirsty recreational desires of hunters. This management includes such tactics as the flooding, burning, and clear-cutting of wooded areas to provide more grazing area for game animals, feeding them in the winter/spring to insure that they will breed more successfully, as well as issuing a disproportionate number of licenses to kill male deer (since their antlers are prized for trophies), resulting in a higher number of female deer who will give birth to even more targets and trophies for hunters. This manipulation of the deer population is designed to maximize the "harvest," rather than minimize the loss of human and animal lives. It also results in *tens of thousands* of deer-vehicle collisions annually in Michigan alone, boosting the costs of insurance in general as well as farmers' crop losses.

It is unsafe for companion animals, farm animals or even humans to be anywhere near the woods during hunting season. People have been killed, while on their own property, by hunters who mistook the property-owner's white mittens for a whitetail deer or because they were careless enough to venture outside *their own home* without wearing hunter orange. It seems the burden of proof that one is *not* a deer, or other target animal, rests with the public, not with the hunters. Few hunters who have killed or maimed a person, whether another hunter or an innocent bystander, have ever been charged with a crime (after all, "accidents will happen").

A Hunting and Trapping They Will Go

"Guns of Autumn," the 1975 CBS hunting documentary, revealed on prime time television just how the woods are managed – lock, stock, and barrel – by gun manufacturers, conservation departments, and other vested interests. Cleveland had asked me if I would be willing to help do an initial "Guns" investigation for CBS at Copper Harbor, Michigan, where nearly-tame bears had become a major tourist attraction at the local dump. Most of the year, they were hand-fed marshmallows and the like, only to then be blasted by hunters on the opening day of hunting season.

Upon receiving my report, CBS made Copper Harbor their first stop. Together with the producer, assistant producer, and three cameramen, we observed the massacre of the unsuspecting bears. In addition to bear hunting in Michigan, CBS viewers witnessed the maiming and death of countless animals, ranging from waterfowl in a "game" management area in Pennsylvania to tame buffalo in Arizona. Throughout the program, hunters boasted of their high-tech armament, introduced hunting guides who would provide them with hard or easy hunts (including firing from an automobile), and even took us to a private hunting preserve near Detroit, where some five hundred animals, including those of many exotic species, were stocked in a one-square mile of fenced-in land, prime targets for the "sportsmen" who were willing to pay to slay.

All the hunters who appeared on "Guns" did so of their own accord. Not one person filmed seemed uncomfortable with what they were doing and, technically, not one of them did anything illegal! Still, hunters and their cronies whined that CBS had been duped into filming an anti-hunting piece. I found this particularly amusing since, long after my involvement in the filming at Copper Harbor, I had asked the producer of "Guns" if I was going to like the final result. He replied that he didn't know because it showed both sides, fifty-fifty. I felt that had to be an improvement since before then, the animals' side was lucky to get five percent. I earned the dubious distinction of having my name appear in the *National Rifleman*, magazine of the NRA, for my part in the Copper Harbor investigation.

The "Guns" exposé set the hunting fraternity on its backside. Indignant hunters, with the help of the Michigan United Conservation Clubs, filed a federal lawsuit against CBS when they were unable to block the showing of "Guns." They sued for libel and slander, maintaining that there was a conspiracy by CBS "to vilify all hunters." I don't consider consulting *both* sides of an issue a conspiracy. The only reason the show was so offensive to them was that it showed the truth. Having personally observed one segment with the CBS crew, I knew the show was not biased. What the public saw on TV was what the hunters themselves presented for filming – hunting as it really is, and it is *not* pretty. In my opinion, MUCC and the other plaintiffs knew they didn't have a valid case. Their lawsuit was simply a ploy to spread more hunting propaganda and to collect even more hunters' money for their cause. Justice prevailed for the animals: MUCC's case was dismissed. The judge ruled, among other things, that the suit could result in the public receiving even *less* information about topics of general concern!

Because the number of hunters in this country is gradually declining, its supporters have launched a massive national campaign to save their industry by trying to recruit women and children into their ranks in a vain attempt to neutralize public opposition. Presently, thirty states actually offer organized children's hunts, with one state's minimum age being six, while several others have no minimum age. Some states are experimenting with projects that match children from non-hunting families with hunters who serve as mentors. Classes in hunter education serve to recruit children into sport hunting. In thirty-seven states, such classes are offered *in public schools, on school time, and with public money*. They are often presented (or, more correctly, misrepresented) under the guise of conservation or wildlife management, and include videos and curriculum units provided to teachers at little or no cost, except to the taxpayer. (*Statistics*, The Fund for Animals, 200 W. 57th St., New York, N.Y. 10019)

The hunting industry and other monied animal exploiters help support the media through their advertising revenues. Since the animal rights movement doesn't have this financial clout, we can become an easy target with which to sell news. It should be noted that those of us in the trenches include teachers, engineers, attorneys, homemakers, nurses, doctors, ministers, office professionals, truckers, actors, psychologists, business people, artists, factory workers, writers, students, law enforcement officers, athletes, and even some policy makers whose focus is on more than just personal gain or bandwagon causes.

One of the most glaring examples of media bias can be found in virtually every newspaper, large or small: the "Outdoor" section. This type of column is supposedly devoted to environmental and conservation issues, as well as to a variety of outdoor sports from boating to skiing to backpacking. It is most often used, however, to sing the praises of hunting and trapping, although *less than ten percent of the population actually engages in such pursuits.*

Woe to the reader who may not share the outdoor columnist's enthusiasm for blood sports. The only recourse is to write a letter to the editor, which may or may not be published; and if it is, it may be edited in such a way as to omit or misrepresent much of its content and intent. If the letter writer is "fortunate" enough to gain the attention (i.e. the wrath or scorn) of the outdoor columnist, there may often follow yet another column devoted to taking the letter-writer to task, without equal space for rebuttal.

    A former outdoor writer from a local paper was infamous for castigating anyone who suggested that hunting and trapping were not "sports," and went so far as to suggest he would set up a "forum" in a public place to debate Cleveland Amory on the subject. Realizing anything this writer set up would be stacked in the hunters' favor, Cleveland offered to share his time on an upcoming TV show to debate the merits of his position. Such a public venue would insure that everyone in Southeastern Michigan could see and hear it. It was no surprise that the outdoor writer gave some lame excuses for wheedling out of the station's invitation. Not to be deterred, Cleveland, during the subsequent "debate" on WXYZ's *Dennis Wholey AM Detroit Show*, appeared on the program and wore (literally) "two hats" (or at least one, a pith helmet which he perched atop his head when playing the role of the outdoorsman). The program was hysterically humorous, and yet oh so true. For every argument Cleveland would pose, his pith-pated counterpart would mouth one of the "party lines" (for example, "We kill animals to save them," or "Hunting is a bonding experience with nature."). The audience loved it, all the typically debatable issues were covered, and the absentee guest must have realized that he couldn't even begin to compete with Amory without his newspaper column to hide behind.

    Another outdoor writer described his technique for desensitizing his daughter (and, presumably, other children) to the suffering and death of animals: "{She} was two when she watched a hunting party in Texas take the hams and backstraps from a pair of deer we had shot – blood running all over the tailgate of the jeep as she played in the rocks at our feet. She watched quite happily. You have to start them out as soon as practicable – after they've gotten some language, but before any fairy-tale-based fears or prejudices about the natural world set in." (*Sports Afield*, Dec. 1994)

Many hunters argue that they love wildlife and kill animals only to save them from disease and starvation. Yet, instead of killing the sickly animals for whom they pretend to be so concerned, they most often kill the healthiest "trophy" animals they can find, thus weakening the gene pool. Those of us who disagree with hunters should be thankful they dislike us so, since they have a strange way of showing love!

If it hadn't been for my personal exposure to blood sports such as hunting, I might not have developed such a strong aversion to them. My husband once took me pheasant hunting and as I downed my first (and last) bird, I was struck by what a cruel and senseless act hunting was. Take away life and you take away all that any creature has. In later years, when designing a bumper sticker for The Fund, I came up with the popular slogan, "Killing for Recreation is Obscene," which, along with The Fund's "Support Your Right to Arm Bears," is a perennial favorite.

In Michigan and several other states, hunters and their cronies in the legislature have managed to push through hunter harassment laws. With all the danger that hunters pose to humans and animals alike, Michigan's DNR (Department of Natural Resources or, as some call it, the "Department of Nuts with Rifles") has chosen to protect the hunters' *feelings* instead of the *safety* of the public and the animals. Under these laws, a hunter can legally shoot an arrow through a deer's eye, but I can't approach that hunter and say, "I don't think you should shoot that arrow into that deer."

One of the first cases of hunter harassment that went to court in Michigan involved several anti-hunters led by Heidi Prescott of The Fund for Animals. They were all arrested on the first day of firearms deer season while on public grounds at a state recreation area. They were later released, but only because the hunters who brought charges against them were found to have illegally started to blast away before daybreak, a case of "premature discharge." Of course, hunters always defend themselves by characterizing anyone among them who breaks the law as a "slob" hunter. *Amazing* how many slobs there are, and all of them toting deadly weapons!

It is particularly repugnant that certain segments of the hunting "klan" continually try to legalize dove-hunting in Michigan. Thus far, public opinion has kept them from pushing their agenda through our legislature. One hunter wrote to me, expressing a very common sentiment among hunters and non-hunters alike. "Dove hunting is a disgrace to sportsmen and only amounts to a form of target practice." I maintain that for food, it is ludicrous; for sport, a sad commentary; and for any reason, unnecessary.

In addition to the many abuses inherent in hunting, the trapping, ranching, and factory farming of animals for fur is rife with cruelties. Leghold traps are indiscriminate, also ensnaring those termed by some as nuisance animals such as cats, dogs, and birds. Trappers are required by most state laws to check their traplines every twenty-four hours. This law, however, is virtually unenforceable, given the out-of-the-way spots most traplines are run, the shortage of law enforcement officers, and the low priority such laws are accorded by state officials. It is not uncommon to find trapped animals who have obviously been ensnared for days, yet are still alive and suffering terribly.

As a Fund investigator, I uncovered many such horrors, including a raccoon which had *all four legs* entangled in leghold traps. The trapper's only concerns were that the raccoon wasn't rabid, since it had bitten him, and that he would get the pelt back after the animal was destroyed. Another case involved a

IS YOUR INSENSITIVITY SHOWING?
... Or is your apathy?

Perhaps you are just one of the many who have never bothered to know just how furs get from the live animals to the merchant's racks.

And if you are satisfied when fur sellers say animals are "ranched" or "not endangered," you may wish to ponder just how "humane" ranching really is, and why there is such a fight to keep from banning the cruel leghold trap method of killing fur-bearing animals.

Those furs that may have seemed attractive before can become an embarrassment once you are aware.

So to save you from embarrassment and to save the animals their skins, think again before contributing to their suffering for your vanity.

The Fund for Animals

Drawing by Bill Shurtliff.

dog caught in a leghold trap for approximately *ten* days, during which time she gave birth to a litter of pups. The dog's leg had to be amputated and the pups destroyed because of the terrible shape they were in. Mary Tyler Moore, then a Fund national chairperson, cited these gruesome findings in federal hearings on trapping legislation.

Trappers insult our intelligence with their argument that animals "fall asleep" in traps. *Obviously the only thing asleep is the trappers' conscience!* There can be *no* humane way to obtain fur, nor any justification for wearing such a cruelty-stained garment.

One of my close friends, Dianne, is married to a successful self-made businessman. She realized that to some in her position, furs might express the *image* of material success, but still they were no measure of true happiness. One evening, while dining with three other couples, Dianne noticed she was the only woman not wearing the typical executive wife's "fur uniform." Being married to auto executives, one of whom had a special involvement in the annual Detroit Auto Show held at Cobo Hall, the other women began discussing the show and the "terrible fur protesters." (That year, there was a fur show and fur sale being held at Cobo at the same time as the Auto Show, but with no official connection to it.) This commentary caused Dianne's husband to laugh, "Yes, my wife was one of those protesters." You can imagine the shock on everyone's faces. Dianne added, "We were merely chanting BUY CARS, NOT FURS." At this point, the executive who was involved with the show burst out laughing as well, realizing how much sense this made. After all, these protesters were turning out to be people much like themselves, but with a different definition of success. Dianne went on to emphasize that furs were becoming passé, as well they should be. Dinner continued on a more civilized note, with considerable food for thought.

The following year's Auto Show again coincided with a fur sale at Cobo Hall. Furriers claimed that many coats on display were damaged by bubble gum, allegedly by those in the animals rights movement. I suspect that since fur sales were down due to increased public awareness of the industry's many cruelties, it was a ploy by the sellers to collect insurance on overstocked furs. Since no culprits were ever discovered, the furriers' claims remain unfounded and, most likely, self-serving.

Now that the fur industry can no longer hide its horrors from the public, it tries to tout furs as *energy efficient* in an effort to seek the environmental high ground. However, a Fund study done in the early nineties scientifically refutes furriers' claims that animals are an economically practical, renewable natural resource, supposedly unlike synthetic materials. "Furs are an expensive 'status symbol.' Like other 'status symbols,' they are unnecessary and costly by any standard. The simple fact that they are expensive is a direct indication of the amount of energy involved in their production. It is usually true that what costs more in terms of energy is what costs more in dollars." (The Fund for Animals, *Animal Furs: Trapped or Ranched: An Energy Waste*, 1991)

Furriers, realizing their business is fighting for its very existence, have now taken to arguing that furs should be a matter of personal choice. While we support people's right to choose, we urge them to take the time to study the issue and to make an informed and, we hope, *humane* choice.

Following are excerpts from some of my most memorable correspondence regarding hunting:

> As longtime animal rights advocates who sometimes

lose heart when faced with human cruelty and insensitivity, we have had occasion to regain a measure of faith in the power of reason and humaneness. A friend of ours recently shared a very gratifying experience with us, an experience which we, in part, brought about. This friend was raised in a family of hunters. His father is a big game hunter. Our friend, while opposed to such hunts, was a deer and duck hunter, true to Michigan outdoorsy tradition. Although respectful of our views, he nevertheless remained unconvinced of the "error of his ways." A short time ago, when he and his wife moved out of state, we asked him to do us (and himself) one favor – read Cleveland Amory's *Mankind?* We loaned him our copy (truly an indication of friendship and trust, since it was our autographed hardbound copy!). Approximately a month later, we received a letter from him, from which we quote: "Our last conversation did have an effect on me. I have read *Mankind?* and now feel like a real ass. I have written Amory and joined The Fund for Animals. So your perceptions were right on and you've won a convert. Amory's book is excellent." Thank you, Ms. Dixon, for your constant encouragement.

–Gregory & Carolyn Smith

Howard Brickner, a Fund volunteer, humorously described his experiences at The Fund for Animals' information booth at the annual Art Fair:

> I had the privilege (?) of talking with one of the true patriots, nature lovers, and conservationists of our

times – the "sport" hunter. Upon approaching our booth, he declared that we weren't really against sport hunting, were we? "After all – wait a second – let me get my official NRA Handbook out here – yes, here it is: I hunt deer to keep them from starving to death because there are so many." I stated that was very admirable, especially since the deer he killed wouldn't ever have to worry about starving to death again. I told him that management was merely artificial propagation of a few game species to the exclusion of others. "Prop-a-what?" he intoned. "Never mind," I said, "just realize that were it not for a few wealthy gun lobbies run of, by, and for the gun manufacturers, some potentially good environmental laws benefiting *all* animals might eventually pass the legislature." The hunter's smile by now was beginning to fade. "Well," he said, "sport hunting groups do a lot in the way of habitat preservation." "Great, all the better to kill more," I said. "Funny it's only for 'game' species. Have your so-called conservation hunting groups done anything to protect the wolf, the whale or help stop baby seal clubbing or prevent the torture of animals caught in steel leghold traps?" He shrugged those off as non-issues and out came his NRA manual. "Many men who hunt are just communing with nature and having a good time," he read. "Besides," he ad-libbed, "we're poor and need the meat." I asked him how much it cost for his last hunting trip. "Oh, about $80 for the rented car, $20 for gas and ammo plus extras for overnight accommodations at a nearby Holiday Inn." (Expensive meat, I thought). "How'd ya like the meat?" I queried. "Well, to tell ya the truth, we got us a big one. Antlers must 'a bin eight feet long. Well, d'ya ever gut a big one? Messy job. Why bother? Got me a head o'er the mantle piece. Besides, thar' was a mighty fine restaurant right in the Holiday Inn."

Another writer, Greg Gorney, proposed a novel solution to our country's military demands:

> Although many citizens do not support a draft, those who do argue that our all-volunteer forces are simply not adequate. The troops, they say, are not all that intelligent, lack coordination, and lack that killer instinct. THE SOLUTION: Draft hunters (and for an indefinite term, I might add). The benefits are many. Having already developed a love of the kill, hunters would not have to be trained for it. It would give us more troops and although the coordination level would stay about the same and the intelligence level might sharply drop, the killer instinct would most certainly be there. Currently, there are close to twenty million hunters in the country and they're breeding like flies ! Of course, if we draft them, their "contributions" to the world of "conservation" and the effects they have had on wildlife would be missed terribly. What would we do if the millions of wild animals and birds that were annually killed, crippled, and maimed by hunters were left alone? How could the public accept the fact that, without hunters, our forests and woods would no longer be dangerous? Since hunters' license money supported "wildlife management" – the burning and flooding of woodlands and manipulation of both habitat and

wildlife to create an overpopulation of certain species – people would have to get used to wildlife being at desirable population levels. And the major accomplishment of the American hunter over the years should not be forgotten: the extinction of several species of wildlife and the endangerment of many others. Once drafted, the only problems I foresee are very minor indeed. The hunters' marksmanship would have to be improved, for shooting at anything that moves is hardly a practical military approach. Also, the hunters' favorite color, orange, would have to be replaced by Army green. Drafting hunters would be a most "sporting" way to end the draft controversy in this country.

Joel Saper, MD, made some excellent points on hunting:

> Recently a hunter suggested that hunting was an integral part of "American heritage," implying that as such, it deserved esteem and preservation. Speak out, he implores! Well, Mr. Sportsman, you *do* speak out: Behold the mighty hunter, bloody carcasses on his car top, bags of rabbits over his shoulder or his grinning face, framed between the antlers of a decapitated buck, as if saying, "Look at me – mighty, virile hunter – I bagged me a deer!" You do speak out – loudly and clearly. You say to all who care that you are brutal, cruel, and primitive. Hunting, part of our heritage? So are witch-hunts, lynch mobs, assassinations, and brutal treatment of minorities. Don't wave our Flag over bloody carcasses and brutally crippled animals, Mr. Sportsman, for it does

not stand for selfish and needless bloodshed, brutal carnage or self-serving platitudes. The Flag could be better served by being wrapped around a national sense of compassion. And, if it is true that hunters really like just being outdoors, then the next time out, why don't you take a camera along and leave your weapons behind? You will find that animals are more civilized to you than you are to them. Hunters often suggest that since animals hunt and kill, and since humans are animals, it is natural for humans to do the same. This absurd analogy seems typical of the other bankrupt defenses used to explain killing for sport and pleasure. Using this analogy, it would be natural for man to defecate, urinate, and copulate on sidewalks. Deriving pleasure from killing suggests a limitation of intellectual, moral, and possibly psychiatric development. To all the "sports" who believe in the naturalness of killing, I reply: Although I am unequivocally opposed to the taking of life, your arguments are so moving that a curious thought came to mind. Instead of hunting and killing animals, you "sports" could hunt each other. After all, the world is overpopulated and people are starving to death. You would spare others that slow and unmerciful end by killing them while they are healthy. What an exhilarating experience it would be to "bag" a few Michiganders or Illinoisans during their season!

10
Voices of Reason

The rights of the helpless must be protected by those who have superior power.
—William James

Animal rights is most commonly defined as the philosophy of allowing nonhuman animals the basic rights that all sentient beings desire: to live a natural life free from exploitation, unnecessary pain and suffering, and avoidable premature death. Animal rights is not about giving animals the right to vote, to marry, to drive a car, and so on, as some of its infantile detractors would absurdly like the public to believe.

Similarly, Ingrid Newkirk, co-founder of PETA (People for the Ethical Treatment of Animals) is continually misquoted as comparing "a rat to a pig to a dog to a boy," thereby suggesting that she and others like her equate the life of a child with that of a rat. What Newkirk *has* in fact said is, "when it comes to *feelings* [emphasis mine] like pain, hunger, and thirst, a rat is a pig is a dog is a boy," meaning they are *all* worthy of concern. Quite a different interpretation than her critics would have us believe.

None of us started out in life knowing everything we should. Most of us ate animal flesh, used cosmetics and toiletries that were tested on animals, maybe even hunted, and never thought twice about rodeos, circuses, and other animal-debasing "entertainment." Some people regard nonhuman animals as lower forms of life and, therefore, less deserving of human compassion. To me, *mercy is indivisible*, though there are always those who would have us think otherwise. It's to their advantage, financially or morally, to perpetuate the myth that an animal is "just" an animal. Well, we are animals, too. We all breathe, think, and feel joy and pain. There are very few people who care only about animals and not about people. I'd trust my humane friends with my life before I would trust someone who doesn't have that depth of caring. While purism is all but impossible, we need to face up to things and do what we can. This step-by-step approach often ignites the spark of compassion in people who might otherwise have been overwhelmed by the bigger picture.

As animal rights activism has increased in recent years, secondary and college students have protested classroom dissection, and have been offered alternatives such as computer modeling. Fur is out, with spokespersons such as Elvira of movie and advertising fame. Even First Ladies Barbara Bush and Hillary Clinton, while not active in the animal rights cause, chose not to wear fur (once considered by many to be mandatory) at their husbands' inauguration ceremonies. Berke Breathed's socially-conscious comics *Bloom County* and *Outland* have tackled animal-eating, hunting, and cosmetics testing on animals in a humorous, yet pointed, way.

We must accept that sometimes people do cruel things because they don't realize they're cruel. The more aware they become, the more likely they are to change. In the process of giving the animal exploiters a bad time, we make friends and we make enemies. There is nothing wrong with that, as long as we make gains . . . and we do. It is certainly not all fun and games, but, all things considered, it's an honorable goal worth pursuing. A person shouldn't just sit around complaining about something without at least trying to change it.

When people ask how I could ever hope to change the attitudes of a dyed-in-the-wool hunter, researcher or other animal exploiter, I remember my son's advice, "Sometimes you just have to wait till they die." Fortunately, we've learned the virtue of patience. I've always tried not to be lulled into the acceptance of something because it is socially or legally condoned. Nearly all human-caused animal suffering is preventable. We must examine every possible nonviolent recourse. There is almost always a path we can be comfortable following if we look for it.

Cynics often try to undermine animal rights with far-fetched arguments such as, "What if broccoli has feelings?" or "If you could only save your child or your dog, what would you do?" The best recourse is to ignore such hysteria and hyperbole and concentrate instead on preventing cruelty whenever and wherever possible. A reply I've used to a hypothetical argument such as the broccoli one is, "I don't know about broccoli (or carrots or whatever vegetable may be in danger), but I do know animals have feelings. On a scale of zero to ten, sentient animals are a ten and broccoli may very well be a negative number." I've refused to become paralyzed into inaction because of ludicrous arguments that don't help anyone except the animal exploiters. As Cleveland puts it, "Man has an infinite capacity to rationalize his own cruelty." No caring person should let the animal exploiters get away with such lame justifications for their behavior.

> ***Blessed are the merciful; for they shall obtain mercy.***
> —Jesus

In my work on behalf of the animal cause, which I have discovered to be an education in politics, religion, and you name it, I came to the realization that many people were disenchanted with their religion due to its general disregard for the animals. The Judeo-Christian tradition generally holds that humans have dominion over animals, that they are at the mercy of humanity's pleasure. What is overlooked by many is the Bible's admonishment that humankind's dominion is actually a stewardship over the natural world.

I receive a great deal of correspondence on this issue of animals and religion. One letter in particular summarized what many people feel. "I am disillusioned by all the various churches that preach only of kindness to our fellow man. This is all well and good, but I have yet to find a minister or church who interprets this to include four-legged or two-winged creatures – *all* living creatures. Do you know of any churches or ministers who do include animals as part of their religious beliefs?" Queries such as this helped to convince me that an organization was needed to address the issue.

Friend and author Lewis Regenstein held a similar belief that religion, with its doctrines of kindness and mercy, needed to be reunited with an overall compassion for animals. To achieve this, he and I established the Interfaith Council for the Protection of Animals and Nature (ICPAN). ICPAN helped make the natural connection between religion and spirituality and animal rights. This message was well-received. ICPAN quickly grew so large that my continued involvement would necessarily affect my Fund work. I chose to turn my duties over to Lew, the president of ICPAN. He wrote to acknowledge that, "At your request we reluctantly accept your resignation from the Board. It has taken two men to replace you and even so, I'm not so sure we'll be back to full strength! There's no one who has done more for animals and for ICPAN and me than you have. You have more guts and courage and determination than anyone else I know."

No matter what spiritual beliefs one holds, everyone has the potential for divine guidance. By tapping into it and by reassessing our vision of stewardship, we will inevitably make the world a better place for all creatures.

After all, whose creatures are we, be we human or non-human? Do any of us "own" each other, or are we all God and Nature's offspring? If those of us supposedly created in God's image can't protect the most helpless of creatures, what hope is there for our own species?

I am in favor of animal rights as well as human rights. That is the way of a whole human being.
––Abraham Lincoln

11
Of Mice and Men

I abhor vivisection. It should at least be curbed. Better, it should be abolished. I know of no achievement through vivisection, no scientific discovery, that would not have been obtained without such barbarism and cruelty. The whole thing is evil.
–Dr. Charles Mayo

Researchers argue that they use animals because they are similar to humans. Animals, like people, have basic needs. Research animals are physically and psychologically deprived and confined while undergoing often unspeakable invasive experimentation. Since few, if any, people would volunteer to have such things performed on themselves, *maybe something is wrong with what is being done!* Contrary to what many researchers would have us believe, federal law does not guarantee protection of research animals from pain and suffering.

Federal law deals mainly with the *housing* of lab animals. As long as researchers can justify an experiment (and they usually can, given the loose guidelines that govern them), they can – and do – withhold pain-relieving medication. At the conclusion of an experiment, the animal is sacrificed (killed) or passed on to another researcher for further experimentation, and *then* sacrificed. However it is handled, experimentation *never* has a happy ending for the animals.

"Animal Care Committees," which are supposed to review prospective animal experiments and prevent unnecessary cruelty and duplication, are most often composed of researchers and veterinarians who police their own ranks. Animal advocates are entitled by law to serve on those committees, yet there are few who actually hold such positions due to opposition from the research community. As with any form of animal exploitation, the exploiters have no incentive to clean up their act without outside intervention. Take away their huge research salaries and other incentives and *then* see how much most of them really care about human health.

If the public knew what was *really* going on behind closed laboratory doors, they would be appalled. Instead, they see only what the vested interests want them to see in order to keep those tax dollars and misguided charitable contributions rolling in. The security measures many labs have taken are designed to keep the public out, not to discourage "militants," as they claim. If you are ever invited into a researcher's lab, you can be certain you will only see what he or she *wants* you to see.

Atrocities are not less atrocious when they occur in laboratories and are called medical research.
–George Bernard Shaw

The list of cruelties performed on animals in the name of science is already far too lengthy, dating back in recorded time to the second century A.D. when the vivisector Claudius Galen practiced such horrors as the severing of non-anesthetized animals' arteries to prove they contained blood rather than air. Then, as now, animals were treated as nothing more than unfeeling "machines" for experimentation. Even in the *supposedly* more enlightened twentieth century, the University of Michigan conducted car crash impact studies on live baboons in the late seventies, although most auto companies had long since ceased to use animals in favor of more sophisticated crash dummies and computer modeling. The Fund, along with a coalition of animal rights activists and church groups, forced the cancellation of the project and thereby rescued "The Baboon Seven," as the survivors came to be known.

My office has become a clearinghouse for countless reports of lab animal abuse. One of the most poignant I received was from a man who quit his job with a pharmaceutical company because he "couldn't stand seeing garbage cans full of beagle carcasses being rolled down the hall, or seeing literally thousands of dogs and monkeys in cages just big enough to breathe in."

My health is as important to me as anyone's is to them. It has become increasingly obvious, however, that animal research is *not* the "magic bullet" it is purported to be. Our apathy regarding animal suffering is itself a mental cancer that only compassion can eradicate. Medical research would benefit humankind far more by stressing disease prevention and by utilizing the many alternatives, such as computer models and tissue cultures.

> **We are healthy only to the extent
> that our ideas are humane.**
> –Kurt Vonnegut

The Physicians Committee for Responsible Medicine (PCRM with Dr. Neal Barnard as president) is composed of doctors and other health professionals who are working toward a different kind of medicine: a shift away from animal experimentation and a renewed emphasis on preventive medicine. Among their goals are a ban on the Draize test, which tests household products in the eyes of rabbits; the non-invasive study of human patients; the critiquing of animal research "models;" the rights of students to decline to participate in dissection and animal labs; reducing cancer and heart disease through diet; and the replacement of animals in such classes as dog labs with alternative methods.

Dr. Michele Dodman, an experienced physician, agrees with PCRM. "I worked exclusively on computer simulations and other models during my studies and was among the top ten in my class. When you find out that aspirin is lethal in rats but not toxic to mice, you learn that animals do not make good research models. If we cannot learn to show kindness and consideration to animals, how are we going to be compassionate towards humans?"

Since most research animals are specifically bred for experimental purposes, there should be, *at the very least*, a nationwide ban on pound seizure (the practice of using stray or abandoned animals in research). Although these unfortunate animals, which the medical establishment *insists* it needs, amount to only a small percentage of the actual number of animals used in research, they still represent a staggering number of animals. Most strays were at one time companion animals, now lost, abandoned or otherwise betrayed. If your companion animal ended up in a lab, *then* would you care? We owe it to our fellow animals to do our best on their behalf.

Ella Wheeler Wilcox eloquently expresses humankind's responsibility to nonhuman creatures:

> I am the Voice of the voiceless
> Thru me the dumb will speak
> Til the deaf world's ear be made to hear
> The cry of the wordless weak
> From street, from cages and from kennel,
> From jungle and stall, the wail
> Of tortured kin proclaims the sin
> Of the mighty against the frail.
> The same Force formed the sparrow
> That fashioned man the king
> The God of the whole gave a spark of soul
> To furred and feathered thing.
> And I am my brother's keeper
> And I will fight his fight
> And speak the word for beast and bird
> Til the world shall set things right.

The following are excerpts from a reader editorial by G.H. Smith in a local paper:

> As a scientist and engineer, I am all too aware of the pitfalls of scientific methodology. It is intended as a means to discovery and change, not an end in itself. Yet the scientist may become so caught up in the scientific mystique that he regards himself as morally and intellectually superior to the layman, and

therefore above reproach. Scientists' most commonly used argument runs thus: How can the antivivisectionist put the life of a mouse above that of a man? Yet this argument, and others like it, are overly-simplistic and detract from the larger issue. Animal experimentation involves suitable "material" from every available species of animals, including man's nearest biological relatives, the other primates. It involves not only animal species specifically lab-bred, but also a vast quantity of stray dogs and cats as well as animals who are trapped in the wild, including primates. This is particularly startling when a number of primate species are currently on the brink of extinction. A number of personal acquaintances who are engaged in biomedical pursuits have admitted to me that a large number of animals are "wasted," partly due to the ignorance or laziness of the investigator, who fails to keep abreast of his colleagues' experiments, and so may needlessly duplicate them. Other investigators rely on government grants to keep them employed. Very "business-like," yet because it is "scientific" business, it is regarded by many as sacrosanct, and therefore above reproach. In addition to the personal motivations of the researchers, there are the scientific justifications, often equally questionable. Animals are used in vast numbers in toxicity tests for new brands of cosmetics and toiletries, pesticides, war materials, and foodstuffs. Animals are even used to study the human sex drive, even though the implications of these studies are obscure or nonexistent. The New York City Museum of Natural History at one time performed experiments involving the sexual mutilation and blinding of male cats in order to study their effects on the tom's sex drive. This research was halted after much public protest. *This is your tax money at work!* While most scientists may not be sadistic, a great many are callous in their attitude toward "lower" animals. Their own vocabulary reveals their lack of compassion. The literature on inducing alcoholism and drug addiction in primates frequently refers to the victims as "monkey junkies." The money spent on such useless studies could be far better spent on more treatment centers for *humans* afflicted with these conditions. Strange that on one hand scientists use animals as "models" because their physiological and psychological reactions so closely approximate man's. Yet these same scientists feel little compunction about exploiting them, rationalizing their behavior by noting that animals lack language, reason, feelings, an immortal soul – whatever separates "them" from "us." Animal life may be regarded by some as "cheap," but that is not sufficient reason to exploit it. As long as the established scientific methodology is not questioned, researchers will not be motivated to alter their centuries-old techniques. It is not a crime nor a sin to question Science. It is *imperative* that we do so, if ever we hope to attain our self-appointed position as the "highest" life form.

C. Weldon, a medical librarian for the University of Michigan, resigned after several years of working in its Experimental Pathology Department. She shared her letter of resignation with The Fund in hopes of alerting others to the fallacies the medical establishment perpetuates:

> I am unable to continue working in a facility where animal experimentation is the order of the day. Prior to my working here, I had given little thought to the practice of vivisection (partly because I did not realize the extent of it within the scientific community; partly because I, like most people, had been conditioned to accept it, however uncomfortably, as a necessary evil). I do not take my job lightly and consequently do not submit this resignation without a great deal of thought. Much of this thought has been provoked by my exposure to the literature of the field. A great many of the experiments appear to be repetitious, of questionable value, and completely lacking in concern for the animal "models" they employ (e.g. isolating living monkey brains from their bodies, simplifying techniques for blinding small animals, etc.). The callousness of the many investigators and others I have observed violates, if not any existing legal code, certainly the moral strictures that should govern the "higher" animals. I refuse to yield to charges (many in the medical literature) of sentimentality, emotionalism, anthropomorphism, "zoophilic psychosis," misanthropia, "Bambiism," *ad infinitum*. I am not motivated by a disregard or dislike for the human race. Rather, I believe that humans will truly be the "higher" animal only when they are willing to extend equal consideration to other species, and when people such as yourselves direct your considerable energies toward finding suitable experimental alternatives.

12
The Good News: We're Not Going Away

True goodness requires us to respect the lives of all creatures. No one may shut his eyes, and regard as non-existent the suffering of which he spares himself the sight.
–Albert Schweitzer

    I hereby dedicate my *Prophecy Epitaph* to animal exploiters such as the composite "J. Tedly Fuggerhodge."

> Here lies J. Tedly Fuggerhodge,
> Who fought so vehemently
> To do away with animals
> In the sights of guns, and arrows,
> In leghold traps,
> In horrible research experiments,
> In inhumane decompression chambers,

> And other cruel inhumanities.
> May he fade forever into the sunset
> That the innocent may live in peace.

As difficult as the animal cause can be, the rewards are immensely meaningful. Like mountain climbing, one does it because it's *there* – a seemingly insurmountable mountain of man-made cruelty that we must tackle.

My way of life is a conscious choice as well as a choice of conscience. I thank God I have been able to do all that I have. I hope you, too, will consider contributing your much-needed efforts. A good fight on behalf of animals is one of the noblest sports this world offers. If the animals could talk, they would surely thank you.

Some Ways You Can Help Animals

- *Convince people to have their dogs and cats spayed or neutered.*
- *Tell a pet shop owner you would prefer they not sell live animals.*
- *Support an effective animal rights organization such as The Fund for Animals and/or your local humane shelter.*
- *Participate in fundraising events for at least one animal group.*
- *Write a letter to newspaper editors and politicians expressing your view in defense of animals.*
- *Ask local business owners who support rodeos or other forms of animal entertainment with advertising to withhold their support and withhold yours as well by not attending.*
- *Let hunters know what you think of their "sport."*
- *Encourage a friend to join an animal rights organization.*
- *Check companion animals for current ID tags and shots.*
- *Take time to investigate a stray animal and return it to its home or take it to the area humane shelter.*
- *Help distribute humane information literature.*
- *Teach the humane treatment of animals.*
- *Purchase fundraising products from an animals rights group.*
- *Convince someone not to let his or her dog or cat run loose.*
- *Be vocal in defense of any exploited or suffering animal.*
- *Show a presently uninvolved animal lover this list.*
- *Educate people about the cruelty of overbreeding dogs and cats.*
- *Favor a healthy and humane vegetarian or vegan diet.*
- *Teach others about the importance of not purchasing or wearing animal fur. Emphasize suffering caused by leghold traps as well as the cruelties of "ranch-raising."*
- *Learn about and pass on the dire need for research alternatives to end the horrors inflicted on live animals in the name of science.*

Each and every thing you do for the animal cause makes an important difference!

About the Authors

Doris Dixon is Midwest Representative of The Fund for Animals. She was born and educated in Ann Arbor, Michigan, where she currently lives, as does her son, Todd, and their family of companion animals. She has held a myriad of jobs ranging from social director to private investigator. Her contributions to the animal welfare/rights movement have helped usher in a new generation of social awareness. In 1993, Doris received a much-deserved Lifetime Achievement Award from the Washtenaw Citizens for Animal Rights. In 1995, she was named Humanitarian of the Year by the Michigan Federation of Humane Societies and Animal Advocates for her lifelong work on behalf of animals.

Carolyn Smith holds a Bachelor's degree in English Language and Literature and a Master's degree in Library Science from the University of Michigan. She lives in Ann Arbor with her husband, two children, and their beagle and feline friends. She has worked as an editor, librarian, and child welfare advocate, and is a member of The Fund for Animals.

To order, send a check or money order for $9.95 plus $2.00 shipping/handling for single copies to:

> Proctor Publications
> P.O. Box 2498
> Ann Arbor, MI 48106-2498
> (800) 343-3034
> (734) 480-9811 fax

Michigan residents should include 6% sales tax. Please call for wholesale discounts offered to retail stores and to animal organizations. Available through Baker & Taylor and Partners Book Distributors.

> A portion of the proceeds from this book
> will be donated to the animal cause.